Religious Education
and the pupil with learning difficulties

Alan S. Brown

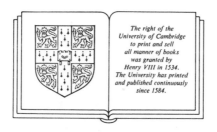

The right of the
University of Cambridge
to print and sell
all manner of books
was granted by
Henry VIII in 1534.
The University has printed
and published continuously
since 1584.

CAMBRIDGE UNIVERSITY PRESS
Cambridge
New York   New Rochelle
Melbourne   Sydney

Published by the Press Syndicate of the University of Cambridge
The Pitt Building, Trumpington Street, Cambridge CB2 1RP
32 East 57th Street, New York, NY 10022, USA
10 Stamford Road, Oakleigh, Melbourne 3166, Australia

First published 1987

Printed in Great Britain at the University Press, Cambridge

British Library cataloguing in publication data
Brown, Alan S.
Religious education and the pupil with
learning difficulties.
1. Learning difficulties   2. Religious education
I. Title
371.9'044   LC4704

ISBN 0 521 33720 8

Contents

Preface

This book is very much a personal quest. It is the result of several years' concern with the way in which the world of Religious Education has passed by the pupil with learning difficulties. To teach such pupils is to concentrate one's mind and energy on what is essential and one's creativity on helping such pupils to express what lies within.

One important point is the variations used in the text to describe pupils who have special needs. Whatever the preferred term by experts (and there does seem to be a lack of uniformity and some rather opaque definitions) in this book terms such as 'slow learner', 'pupil with learning difficulties', etc. are interchangeable. I offer no apology for this – anyone who sits in school staffrooms will hear a rich variety of terms for those pupils who, for whatever reason, do not learn at what their teachers consider to be an appropriate rate.

I must express my thanks to everyone involved but especially Betty Levi and Ivy Peacock – both so imaginative and supportive, to Erica Musty who helped with the resources and to Judy Thursby, Sheila Jack and Gillian Vigne, my colleagues who spent a great deal of time working on the manuscript. And thank you also to all the pupils, teachers and schools who helped in the work, even though their real names are not used in the book. Finally all royalties go to The National Society who supported the work, as one would expect from a Society with over 175 innovative years promoting education in England and Wales.

Alan Brown
The National Society's RE Centre
23 Kensington Square, London W8 5HN

Introduction

How many times have you taken your driving test? Has anything you have put up on the wall fallen down? How often have the instructions of a complex piece of equipment been read to you and you *still* don't understand how to make it work? Why do the instructions that accompany a new piece of equipment never tell you basic things – like how to open it? Absurd questions perhaps, but most of us have experienced the difficulty of achieving success; most of us, if not all of us have 'failed' at something; we have in fact been 'slow learners' or have experienced 'learning difficulties' or whatever jargon seems to be appropriate. Yet in so many areas of life it doesn't matter, we can even make a joke of our inability to understand or failure to manipulate some piece of equipment. Our confidence can be reassured from what we achieve elsewhere and compensates for our lack of ability.

This self-image is as crucial to the pupil in the school as it is to the adult, each pupil must feel some compensation that mutes the crashing disappointment of not achieving what one's peers achieve. Schools, however, appear to assess pupils on the ability to achieve a set standard in certain very narrowly defined limits. Learning problems are frequently attributed to the inability of the pupil to read, to write, to pay attention, to behave acceptably; they do not always take into account the ability of pupils in other less 'academic' areas. Motivation and the learning that accompanies it is far more likely to take place if the pupil has a satisfactory image of himself or herself. Like adults they seek for their own credibility and to experience consistent failure makes future failure so much more likely.

In response to this the teacher of remedial, slow learning, educationally subnormal pupils (or whatever name one attaches to them) has to develop a number of complex strategies which are intended to establish what is most appropriate for each pupil. Knowledge is not enough but equally there is no one method which can succeed in all cases – the teacher must be prepared to extemporise and risk new ideas. This is an exciting element in teaching and one that can be strange to some teachers who rely heavily on content or specialise in teaching examination pupils.

Much of the work with pupils with learning difficulties has concentrated on developing their literacy and numeracy skills using a variety of learning methods, including, in recents years, computers. Little has been done in the area of Religious Education and it is legitimate to speculate why that may be the case. When Kenneth Hyde wrote his book *Religion and Slow Learners* (SCM 1969) he based most of his conclusions on the results of questionnaires and statistical analysis. It was, and remains, an interesting book not least because it provides an indictment of the approach and attitudes of some teachers of RE at that time. The pupils on the other hand, if one reads the book carefully, come out of the situation quite well, a conclusion that one suspects was not lost on Kenneth Hyde himself. The book does not look at practical examples of teaching from slow learning groups nor does it grapple with the issues raised by teaching RE in the special school.

Publications since 1969 have occasionally referred to the pupil with learning difficulties but some have become enmeshed in the relationship of Moral Education with Religious Education, being primarily concerned to help pupils make moral choices. Other journals have contained articles written by teachers but have not attempted a systematic study of the issue.

One reason for this may be the turmoil and development in RE during the last twenty-five to thirty years. The essentially Bible based teaching of the 1950s and early 1960s gave way, through the influence of Ronald Goldman and Harold Loukes, to an approach based on life skills – but still fundamentally Christian – as exemplified by the Agreed Syllabus for the West Riding in the mid 1960s. Almost immediately after this came a boom in the study of world religions led by the work at Lancaster and continued through the Shap Working Party until Christianity came to the fore again, but this time from the point of view of a world religion. Personal and Social Development courses seem to suggest a spiral in the RE curriculum whereby one revisits familiar places but the people are different.

Another reason may reflect the insecurity of the RE profession. Protected by law since the Education Act (1944) and subject to criticisms of evangelism and indoctrination, the RE teacher has had to fight hard for recognition on educational grounds. The subject has had to fight continuously to be recognised as an academic subject worthy of proper timetabling and appropriate resources on educational grounds. Consequently concern with the remedial pupil may appear at best a luxury or at worst a recognition that RE has no place in an academic curriculum. This shows a complete inability to recognise the great intellectual exercise and educational vision required to teach a pupil with learning difficulties – the energy has to be channelled into constructing suitable methods and strategies rather than developing content.

These are some of the issues tackled in this book, but unlike Kenneth Hyde's book already mentioned, it approaches the issues through the practical aspect of the classroom. There are no questionnaires, there is no statistical analysis.

About the book

The book is in its main part a description, with some evaluation, of how different teachers in different schools went about teaching RE to a variety of age ranges. Some were trained RE specialists but most were not. Some taught in primary schools, some in middle schools, others in special schools. All were concerned to help their pupils to acquire a better understanding of religion.

Chapter 2 covers a project involving three middle schools and one primary school, in order to cover the 9 to 13 age range. Two of the schools were in London, two were in a rural area. The aims of this project were:

(a) to develop material for the teaching of Religious Education appropriate to the requirements of the 'slow learner'

(b) to assess how different teaching methods in Religious Education can encourage the 'slow learner'

(c) to encourage teachers to look carefully at how Religious Education in the school curriculum may take account of the needs of the 'slow learner'

(d) to explore ways in which the learning and teaching of Religious Education in mixed ability classrooms may meet the requirements of the 'slow learner'

(e) to enable Religious Education to become a medium for developing the skills of the 'slow learner'

There is a sense of cynicism within me which suggests that anyone can make up a collection of aims, but it is extremely difficult to put these into practice in the classroom. It might help to put these aims into perspective if I described some of the problems that lay behind them.

For years, it seemed, work with pupils with learning difficulties in Religious Education had been ignored or developed on an *ad hoc* basis. I hoped, therefore, that if one could take four schools, two from a rural area and two from an urban area, this might provide a useful mix of pupil and teacher attitudes. Initially the idea was that each school would develop a scheme of work for a term, this would then be used in one of the other schools. Obviously modifications would occur but, in theory at least, one might gather together a basic topic with a number of varieties of teaching it. Each class teacher would be able to look at the scheme of the other, take from it what appeared useful and supplement it with their own ideas and resources. It meant that each teacher would have to keep a record of what they did and be prepared to look at the schemes and comments of others.

Looking back it was an extremely ambitious idea – and it did not work. At least, it worked in terms of creating a greater interest in teaching RE to pupils with learning difficulties, and the teachers were certainly pleased to think about what they were doing in concert with others. However, it is very difficult to persuade teachers to take over another teacher's scheme of work: it has tremendous resource implications; it does not fit into the syllabus developed by an individual school; it requires teachers to keep a careful log of what actually happened in the classroom, this is very time consuming, and the teachers did not meet on many occasions so it was impossible to forge a common link. There are other problems too: what is possible in one school may not be so in another owing to timetabling, curriculum policy and so on; teaching methods and strategies can differ radically and in one case the fundamental aim of the RE teacher appeared quite different from the others.

Oddly enough this did not destroy the project nor does it appear to have made the work less valuable. What it did do was to make all the participants realise that reading ideas in books or discussing them round a table is one thing, teaching them in the classroom is another. Pragmatism became the key feature of the work in the schools. One has ideas, all the teachers did, but in the end the issue was one of teaching more effectively, meeting the pupils on their own ground and dealing with classroom problems as they arose.

It was out of this muddle and confusion and the failure to put into practice the original plan that the above five aims evolved. I felt this to be a salutary lesson to all those involved in planning work to be done in schools – it nearly always doesn't work as it was originally planned and if you think it does then something has gone wrong. It has also made me realise that when I read a book, a handbook, or a collection of teaching schemes I must look for the failures. The initial concept of the project failed, though the reader can judge later whether any useful work did emerge, but then all teachers fail, all of us fail, and the unwillingness or inability to acknowledge our failure inhibits our moving forward. As teachers many of us do not like being exposed to our professional colleagues, yet part of the way in which we come to understand the pupil with learning difficulties is by recognising our failure and therefore being more sensitive to theirs. John Holt wrote a book some years ago *How Children Fail* (Penguin 1969). I would like to see the teaching profession become much more honest and open about their *own* failures because in my opinion the pupil's 'failure' can be related to the teacher's failure.

In the second chapter each school will be described in some detail and an account of the different teaching methods given. In one of the schools, the primary school, I did most of the teaching myself, in the other schools I acted as a consultant and sat in lessons teaching only occasionally. Although the examples have been drawn from primary and middle schools they can easily be adapted with a little initiative and ingenuity and used at all levels regardless of age.

The third chapter was brought about by a number of teachers in ESN(M) and (S) schools, and a school for the delicate, pointing out that the requirements of the Agreed Syllabus in RE applied to them too, so what could they do? A large group of teachers in special schools pooled their ideas and experiences in order to create a handbook of what can be achieved in the classroom. The age range continued up to 16. Teachers in the state secondary sector could well benefit from adopting and adapting some of the methods and ideas – to one who has not taught in a special school the differences at first appear enormous but, in fact, there are enormous similarities related to attention span, reading problems, environment, motivation etc. This chapter forms a substantial part of the book because it is essentially practical.

The fourth chapter takes a rather different look at teaching the pupil with learning difficulties in the secondary school. We often look at education 5–16 as a whole yet most teachers recognise the tremendous division between primary and secondary school, even between middle and secondary school. This chapter does not look at specific teaching programmes and is not practically based as are the two previous chapters.

What it does attempt to do is to argue that, if these pupils are to get a better deal in the secondary school, then there are fundamental changes that must take place in the curriculum and in teacher attitudes. There are some general points about pupils with learning difficulties and a short final part on how resources may be used.

Finally the conclusion considers evaluation, setting out what conclusions one may draw, though if you do skip rapidly to the end it may be a disappointment, for there is no easy answer, no pot of gold. This book contains the blood, sweat, tears and commitment of teachers and, while you may not necessarily read it from beginning to end, you do have the chance to dip into the middle. The appendices list some resources you might find helpful, some addresses where you can obtain information and a booklist for those who might wish to read further (and more entertaining) books.

Before moving to the more practical aspects it is worthwhile trying to reach some understanding of what two of the basic terms might mean. 'Slow learner', 'pupil with learning difficulties', 'remedial pupil' – we need to consider what teachers mean by 'slow learner' and its implication for the pupil. We also need to consider what the aims of RE are, without becoming too bogged down in the jargon which bedevils all educationalists.

1

The relationship between the pupil with learning difficulties and Religious Education

What is meant by learning difficulties?

Labels, when attached to people, assume a formidable power – for good or ill – and all of us must be aware of being labelled in a manner that might result in anything from humour to depression. All teachers who deal with pupils who have a learning problem must feel some discomfort at using the range of terms available to them (outside the staff room at least). 'Remedial' classes, 'pupils with learning difficulties', 'slow learners', 'ESN' all carry pejorative overtones which place the pupil in a disadvantageous light. New terms for old concepts do not solve the problem for such terms still refer to pupils who are considered to have failed within the education system and do not always acknowledge that it may well be the system that has failed the pupil. No one likes to be associated with failure, yet some of our educational institutions reinforce failure through their curriculum policies and their streaming of pupils.

This creates a classic 'Catch 22' situation in which pupils respond to the expectation of the teacher/school, and because they respond in a fashion which matches that of teacher/school they are classified as 'slow learners'. It makes it extremely difficult to raise teacher expectation and pupil self-image, because pupils who fall into this category are classified as essentially different from mainstream pupils. There is a facile belief, unfortunately not yet buried, that all pupils in remedial classes or in special schools have low IQs. In fact the issue is far more complex than many teachers appear to believe, but then life itself is always more complex than any of us would wish to believe.

This book is intended as a handbook of advice and ideas for teachers of pupils of all ages and of all schools, and it is therefore inappropriate here to explore the more philosophical and psychological definitions of an inability to learn quickly and effectively, important though these undoubtedly are.

The concern is more pragmatic – how do teachers define the slow learner? What criteria do they invoke when making such assessments? Generally speaking it appears that many teachers make their assessments on personal judgement, rather than any external evaluation of the pupil's ability. When asked how they decided which pupils had problems learning the replies of teachers fell into four broad categories:

1   The most popular classification could be described as *relativism*, because there always appeared to be a pupil, or group of pupils, of lesser ability in every class and every teacher could easily identify the pupil who did not learn at the same rate as the others. This identification of a pupil, or some pupils, as having learning difficulties appeared to take place regardless of the average level of ability or attainment of the class as a whole. All who teach can recognise this situation, particularly when it is applied across the curriculum for pupils who have the label 'slow learner' in one class may demonstrate their ability in another. There will be complex reasons for this and teachers need to be sensitive to the background of each pupil as well as pausing to reflect on the nature of the pupil-teacher relationship. In mixed ability teaching too, the teacher is required to re-think teaching methods and strategies for pupils who may respond positively to one approach while rejecting another. The ability of teachers to use a variety of teaching methods and to be able to reassess value judgements of the pupils' achievements are two of the most necessary professional skills.

2   Some pupils fall behind the normal expectation of the teacher; this is not relativism, it is probably a variant of *under-achievement*. This can be a subtle method of including the lazy or disruptive pupil within the broad category of 'slow learner'. In one of the schools used in the project the most disruptive pupil, the one who caused most 'problems' in the lesson, was put with the pupils who had learning difficulties whereas he was in fact extremely bright – he just didn't fit into the system. As in all human relationships teacher and pupil meet on a number of levels, the relationship is not normally one purely of academic interest. The personal constructs that are exchanged mean that the assessment of a pupil and the evaluation of ability contains a

range of things – politeness, dress, behaviour, neat work, pleasant manner and so on, in addition to all the unseen signals which flash between humans when they talk and relate to each other. As these constructs are assimilated and understood so teacher and pupil develop a better understanding of each other. It is very important that teachers are sensitive to this interaction and are able to suspend personal feelings when making any assessment of a pupil's ability. If they are unable to do this then some pupils will be classified 'remedial' or 'subnormal' simply because they have not met teacher's expectation or not been socialised into the requirements of the educational institution.

3   One head teacher agreed that the school should not be involved in any such evaluation of the pupil's ability, though the school should be helping the pupil to identify where he or she had most difficulty. She suggested that the middle school could do no other because pupils entered from such a variety of experiences in the first school. So in her school no pupil could (or should) be classed as a 'slow learner', for the prime task of the middle school was to sort out the remedial issue handed on from the first school. It was almost impossible to think of how to term this approach, 'ostrich-head-in-the-sand'? However, on reflection the word *equality* appeared to be appropriate because the head teacher was suggesting that each pupil presented an equal challenge to the teacher, the assessment was not the pupil's ability but the ability of the teacher to respond to the requirements of the pupil.

    As an aside, it did seem to be an odd philosophy that the principal aim of the middle school was to 'sort out' the vagaries of the first school. This view has the merit of trying to suspend judgement and making teachers take responsibility for the pupil's learning as well as their own teaching. It could be argued, however, that it is too idealistic. For good or ill people tend to classify others and teachers are no exception when evaluating pupils. In addition, evaluation of the pupils did take place in the school – the Local Education Authority required pupils to be banded on leaving in order to ensure a range of ability in the upper schools, so regardless of the idealism of equality the pragmatism of the school system weighed heavily in the end.

4   The last category could be termed *responsibility*. A number of teachers were passionately committed to the inclusion of all pupils in one classroom except possibly for the pupils in ESN(S) schools. The responsibility for the learning of all pupils was to be shared by teacher and pupil. This view has a direct and powerful effect upon teaching

strategies and teaching methods, for the pupil's learning problem may be related to a physical handicap which in turn could affect his or her mobility. To have one's academic achievement impaired by a physical handicap is unfortunate to say the least and suggests such pupils need to be over-compensated. A reflection on a variation of teaching method can benefit a whole class, and even the school, for it can produce a whole range of advantages for all pupils. One school had experimented by teaching RE using team-teaching. Because of its obvious success the team-teaching approach was extended to other year groups throughout the school encouraging more staff in the school to become involved with teaching RE.

From this it appears that, in general, a 'slow learner' is a pupil who reads with difficulty or not at all; writes partly or not at all; has a very short attention span and is often badly behaved or at least causes some disruption. In none of the schools did there appear to be any clear criteria by which the pupil's ability was normally assessed.

This is not the place to speculate as to why some pupils have difficulty learning nor is it possible to review the considerable literature on the subject. Many teachers do not have time to read all the literature anyway; they work under tremendous emotional pressure. They work closely with colleagues of course, but most teachers spend most of the day in a room with anything from 12 to 35 pupils and cannot avoid forming close relationships with them. Even the special school teacher with perhaps a class of 10 pupils will form an individual relationship with each pupil that does not always allow time to stand back and analyse all the possibilities for the slow progress of a pupil. Diagnosis can be difficult for there can be a variety of reasons. Two specific examples occurred during the period of the project. In one school, while making a film, a girl said she could barely see through the view-finder, a sight defect discovered at the age of eleven which must have hindered her progress during her school life. Similarly, a boy was discovered to see certain letters inverted in a word which must have explained in part at least his reading difficulties. Teachers of all ages and classes have to be so alert that one has to respect the professional expertise required; they have to recognise that the pupil who does not understand immediately may have a physical problem.

The question of diagnosis has interesting implications if one remembers the powerful influence of Piaget on teacher training institutions over the last twenty to thirty years. (This influence extended directly into the field of Religious Education during the 1960s through the work of Ronald

Goldman.) Having taught in an institute of higher education for almost ten years it seemed the importance of Piaget was so central that others were pushed to the sidelines. Piaget contributed immensely to our understanding of the whole area of child development, but he appears to have paid relatively little attention to the varieties of assessment by which a child's understanding of ideas and concepts may be measured.

To put it crudely, and therefore perhaps not quite accurately, if a pupil has great difficulty reading and writing does the teacher assume that the pupil 'knows' very little? The vast range of assessment procedures available to the teacher depend very heavily on the skills of reading and writing. How can the teacher be sure that a pupil lacking the skills has acquired knowledge and/or understanding? Does a pupil 'know' something if they lack the skills to articulate that knowledge in the accepted formal manner? Piaget's theory of the stages of child development begs all sorts of questions which may not be dealt with here, though they will have relevance later in the book. One of the crucial issues among contemporary educationalists is how effectively assessment procedures monitor the pupil's knowledge and understanding. If the western world today lives in a 'post-literate age', as Marshall McLuhan claimed, then there ought to be other means of developing a profile of a pupil's achievements.

It is likely that pupils learn a great deal more than they are ever invited to express formally, and when the invitation is offered it is invariably, with the exception of special schools, through the media of reading, writing, drawing etc. Knowledge and intelligence are usually tested through the ability to respond in an accepted fashion – a formal structure. This is the area where the teaching profession has largely failed to recognise its responsibility to the slow learner. The exception to this must surely lie within the special schools where the innovation and improvisation of teachers continues to open up new experiences for their pupils. These schools are prepared to recognise qualities which do not normally receive adequate recognition in the state school; they also have something to contribute to curriculum design, which in secondary schools appears geared to the academic pupil.

So what finally is a 'slow learner'? Is it simply a pupil who lacks the intelligence of their peer group? Is the term a relative one, as all teachers look for a hierarchy of ability in their pupils? But, as we have seen, these definitions are all conditioned by a variety of factors. Here we have to lapse into jargon, for perhaps *wholeness* is a helpful term. If we are to make judgements about any person we need as much detail as possible from as many sources as possible and even then we will have an imperfect picture.

It is rather like a three-dimensional jigsaw where some pieces are missing and there is no completed picture to act as a guide. Each stage is provisional and every assessment of progress is made in the situation at the moment – a 'whole' view as far as is possible but the complete picture is beyond everything.

Where teachers have a group of pupils for a whole year they are in a better position to offer a provisional assessment of wholeness. In the secondary school where assessments can be more crucial to a pupil's immediate future *provisional* often becomes *arbitrary*. But, before second-ary teachers rise in protest, they do liberate the pupil from the year of misery with a teacher where the pupil–teacher relationship has failed. In secondary schools with well organised pastoral systems the whole pro-visional picture may be more conclusive.

What about Religious Education?

There is so much debate about the primary aim of Religious Education that consensus appears impossible. In my view and for the purposes of this study the aim of RE is:

> to help the pupil to understand religion

in other words, a purely educational aim. For, if RE is to claim its rightful place in the curriculum of any school, it must do so on educational grounds and not hide behind the legal provisions of the Education Act (1944), nor exploit its protected position and the integrity of the pupil by becoming a vehicle for proselytising and evangelism. If it does either of these then the subject loses its educational validity and is no longer a proper subject of study.

It would be naive to dismiss further discussion without some thought on the teacher's own point of view. Some teachers in church and county schools believe that their own religious conviction must be shared with and adopted by the pupils they teach; others do not believe in imposing their views on pupils but assume that pupils do share or at the very least implicitly accept them. Today the majority of teachers of RE take the view that ultimately the pupil has to construct a set of beliefs and values for herself or himself, though these may well be based on accepted religious tradition. The role of the teacher is to stimulate and develop the critical faculties and skills necessary for the study of religion.

The cry of 'indoctrination' is never far from the ear of the RE teacher and indeed it may be the case, in fact it certainly is, that some teachers do use the opportunity to indoctrinate. However, as we shall see later, it is extremely difficult to distinguish between indoctrination in religion and indoctrination in other areas. Much of society indoctrinates the pupil into patriotism, nationalism, the work ethic and morality so one needs to be very careful before pointing the accusatory finger. Indeed the finger may be directed towards the teacher of English, science, history and so on, for each can provide its own exclusive view. It is the case that teachers not specifically trained in RE can be nervous when teaching the subject lest they misrepresent or misinterpret the personal and important beliefs and practices of others.

One interesting and largely unresolved issue arising out of this approach is how to teach RE to pupils who lack the critical faculties so necessary to evaluate the information. How can such pupils distinguish what they are given as information from what they are required to believe or to participate in? Should these pupils be nurtured into a particular faith so they will not have to be critical but simply feel secure?

Religious Education and nurture

These questions do raise an important issue in Religious Education, one that has become increasingly controversial over the last few years. If RE is to be non-confessional and not attempt to assume a faith or to promote a particular religion, it has to avoid the assumption that each pupil has a faith, is looking for a faith or is being brought up in one (normally in much of Britain, Christian). RE is concerned with helping pupils to understand religion, to make them aware of its basic beliefs and to see how these beliefs have been, and are being, expressed through their various practices.

If one can broadly agree with this, and not all teachers of RE would, then there is a close and natural link with the normal and accepted process of education. But it does not allow, nor accept, nurture or growth within, or into, a faith, for that would be the responsibility of the religion itself.

This is all very well, but life is always more complex than one would wish. This complexity surrounds the use of the word 'nurture' and its ambiguity when applied to education as a whole. Firstly, all teachers are, or should be, involved in 'nurture' in some sense of the word for presumably they wish to help pupils develop and attain a maturity and potential that will enable them to play a full part in life after school. The term *in loco parentis* captures this approach to education which cannot be solely concerned with the transmission of information but must be critically involved with the whole life of each individual pupil. All teachers must look back upon pupils they have taught and be able to recognise how they were caught up in the educational process of that pupil. Bonds do develop between teacher and pupil where the teacher becomes fully committed to nurturing the pupil into society as a whole. Anyone who has spent time in school, particularly a remedial class or a special school, can immediately recognise the amount of energy and commitment put into the lesson. All such relationships go far beyond the professional requirements of the teacher for everyone would acknowledge the strong human and emotional ties that must develop. So in this sense the word 'nurture' is appropriate for teachers do nurture their pupils (or many of them do), perhaps not into a religion in the explicit sense, but certainly into the creation and acceptance of shared attitudes and values appropriate both to society and to the individual pupil.

Secondly, it is a fashion to identify Religious Education and Moral Education as being concerned with the same area of the pupil's development. It is assumed by some, from MPs to clergy and on to teachers and parents, that the principal aim of Religious Education is to make the pupils *good*. In one such example an MP in the mid 1980s claimed that more and better RE in schools would reduce football hooliganism. Clearly moral issues have a significant role to play in every religion; in society as a whole the inculcation of moral values, agreed or imposed, which pupils are expected to learn and keep is considered desirable.

For those with such a view the principal aim of RE appears to be a variety of 'cleanliness is next to godliness', an RE devoid of virtually all religious content but training pupils to accept what they see as the essential Christian, Jewish or Muslim message. This is nurture in a different sense from the above because its parameters are so narrow. More important, however, is that the relationship is an essentially human one between the teacher and the pupil: it is personal and emotional. The sense of 'nurture' in the present usage is that of acceptance of values; it is impersonal for it is not based upon the teacher–pupil relationship but upon a set of values that the pupil is required to accept. Whether this can be nurture or not is another question, but the regimentation required appears to disregard the importance of personal example and personal relationships. To some extent of course religions do require acceptance of a set of conventions, it might indeed be argued that this is a function of religion, a sort of institutionalisation of charismatic experience but it does ignore the awkward and disruptive qualities of so many religious leaders, like Moses, Isaiah, Jesus and Muhammad.

My opinion is that the term 'nurture' has outlived its usefulness, if indeed it was ever useful. It may have a use in the broad educational sense but it cannot continue to be attached to Religious Education. The development of effective pastoral systems in virtually every school has meant that nurture cannot be left to the religious educators – and a good thing too. Schools are by their very nature protective environments, they are places where the young are nurtured though it does not always feel like that for pupil or teacher. Teachers have to consider to what end they are nurturing their pupils. Do they wish to make them acceptable and presentable adults? Or do they wish to nurture self-confidence and, indeed, a confidence to face the world beyond the school gate?

So in one sense nurture may be absolute for it is an educational activity common to all teachers. One may argue that the methods adopted by all the religious communities to ensure their children grow up in the faith hardly reflect the normal meaning of nurture – the methods make assumptions and provide information to which the word 'regulation' would be more appropriate.

With specific regard to the pupil with learning difficulties the relationship between RE and nurture is more complex. A quick glance at the Agreed Syllabuses for RE will indicate how important content is. It is important that certain things be taught to the pupils in a balanced syllabus and the Handbooks attached to the syllabuses provide examples of how the content may be taught and hopefully learned. But for a remedial pupil or a pupil with learning difficulties much of the content may be difficult to grasp – it may be not understood or instantly forgotten. If this is the case does the content of RE when taught to such groups matter at all? If the carefully constructed syllabus of RE formulated by a local authority (or anyone else) falls gently to the ground because its mysteries cannot be penetrated by the slow learner then should choices be made on their behalf and should they be educated into a faith? Should the teacher assume that such pupils will be unable to make evaluative judgements and simply teach from a particular point of view so that the pupils will at least have a firm basis of understanding?

The immediate and forceful response to this must be 'no' for a number of reasons:

1   It is patronising to assume that pupils with such difficulties cannot make evaluative judgements. They may lack the skills to communicate them effectively but the teacher has to accept that these pupils enjoy the same rights as any others.

2   It is optimistic to believe that any teacher can do full justice to a religion in the classroom. For example, there are many Christians teaching RE whose views would not be shared by other Christians. One is not therefore presenting pupils with information upon which to make a choice or base a future life, one is helping their understanding.

3   As teachers we can overrate content – we can assume that it helps pupils to make individual choices, and perhaps in some cases it does do so, but human beings often choose a course of action when they are perfectly aware that they are doing something they should not. Sometimes we make decisions apparently on the basis of rational argument, but do we not also make a decision and then rationalise it?

4   The importance of relationships was referred to earlier. How many adults remember much of their school days? Can you think now of what you learned at school? What do you feel now about what you learned at school? Some adults may have spent five or six years learning French but be quite unable to speak it 15 to 20 years later. Was it a waste of time, or was the experience of the learning process a valuable aid to education in its broadest sense? Indeed knowledge seems to expand so rapidly that it is quite likely that much of what adults do remember is now considered to be incorrect.

5   Finally, we have to consider feelings, emotions and the affective area of learning. We learn through our experiences and religions are full of experiences. They seek to transmit and retain these through ritual, festival, liturgy, prayer, worship etc. Pupils of all ability will receive an inadequate understanding of religion if they do not share in this affective area of religion. This is not nurture into a faith, but simply trying to make the pupils sensitive to the signs and sounds of religion. Perhaps the analogy may be made with drama – it is one thing to read a play, it is another to see it acted, and yet another to participate in it oneself. So with religion. If one talks with pupils, particularly the younger ones, they realise that certain events are special. For many Christmas means something special, though the events may be jumbled and confused with pantomimes they *feel* it is different. It is the same with other areas of RE and this is why teaching methods are so critical when teaching the slow learner.

All this may seem a long way from nurture and RE and yet it has a strong bearing upon what and how we teach. It is relatively simple to transmit 'facts' but if we are to make religions come alive to the pupil we have to be prepared to grapple with the tension that exists between education and nurture. Like all teaching, the bland is boring and repetitive, it is the lines around a subject which are of interest. Religion is controversial, it creates barriers and uncertainties yet these are the areas that are so important. Religious Education has to engage the pupil at all levels and all abilities, it will not do so if it assumes content is of sole importance and ignores the integrity of the pupil and the importance of creative tension in the classroom.

Paradoxically therefore content can be both unimportant and yet crucially important for the slow learner in RE. It does not *direct* the pupil, it does not seek to provide information upon which decisions and choices will be made. What it actually does, or should do, is to help the pupil with decisions they have already made or may make in the future. So, for example, a world religions approach would not be primarily designed to teach the pupil about the Sikhs, for example, but would assist them to recognise the integrity of the Sikh religion and the commitment of its followers, in order to appreciate the significance of difference and diversity.

So if nurture has to remain within the grasp of religion it should really be directed towards the creation of awareness and understanding of the importance of religion in the lives of some people. This acts as a bridge between nurture into a faith and nurture into the world outside school.

What should the teacher of the slow learner teach in RE?

The transmission of facts, whether it be a Bible story or the fundamental axioms of Islam, is considered essential by some teachers, but facts are not easy to come by in religion. It is extremely difficult to make a categorical statement in any religion that would be universally agreed by every member of that religion. One can describe what people do – their religious practice – but one cannot assume that the same intent lies behind that practice. So content is not the all-consuming fire of education that some believe and others worry about. This is a criticism not only of some remedial teaching, but of any teaching where the pupil is required to learn a set of facts to no obvious purpose other than to imitate a parrot, rather than developing an awareness of how to understand and deal with people who do, or do not, share one's world view.

More than most, the teacher in the special school or the remedial class has to make sure that what they teach is fun – not a jokey, empty comedy but an enjoyable activity. The motivation of the pupil should not be the threat of external examinations, it should come through the pupil-teacher relationship, the method of learning, variety of activities, the content itself and so on. Enjoyment has to be a key feature. If the primary aim of RE is to help the pupil to understand religion, the secondary aim must be to ensure that the subject is taught in an enjoyable way.

The clarification of the aims of RE is important for it has to stand as a subject separate from the desire to create and sustain the morality of the pupil. The wish to teach a wall-to-wall consensus of moral attitudes can supplant the religious element in RE. One suspects this is because those teachers who feel uncomfortable when teaching about religion can at least make a conscience-free commitment to encourage pupils not to take up anti-social habits. It is not clear why some teachers feel pressured into thinking they have to 'believe' in a religion before they can teach it. It suggests that the educational judgements they apply to other subjects are suspended when teaching about religion. For example, one may not believe in 'slavery' or 'prejudice' but both topics are not uncommon in schools, and how often do teachers who say 'I can't teach anything I don't believe in myself' teach aspects of geography or science which they don't believe in at all.

If clear aims for RE can be established by the school and the individual teacher then the teacher who lacks confidence will at least be teaching within a level of competence. Uncertainty of aims, objectives and content can make it extremely difficult for the pupil to learn anything, consequently teachers have to apply their educational expertise to the subject of religion; they have to apply the imagination and ingenuity that are clearly demonstrated in classrooms across Britain.

When teachers feel confident and reassured in what they teach the teaching methods expand, activities become varied and the atmosphere is relaxed, however insecurity breeds fear and a lack of confidence. As many remedial class teachers and teachers in special schools are not normally trained RE specialists they must consider carefully where their expertise lies and apply this to each subject. This brings us back again to the issue of content and method.

Subjectively, the evidence from the project suggests that pupils learn a great deal more than they are ever invited to articulate and when they are invited, it is through writing, drawing, reading etc. It seems to me that this is where the teaching profession, from its chalk-face teachers to its academics, has consistently failed to recognise its accountability to the slow learner. It seems now, more than ever, that the onus is on the teaching profession to create a means whereby assessment of the slow learner is considerably broadened and credit is given for skills not normally recognised in the mainstream educational world. It raises questions too, not only about assessment but about curriculum design. For whom is the curriculum designed? For the staff or for the pupils? If it *is* designed for the pupils, for which pupils and how does it cater for the others? In mixed ability classes it is not easy to cater for the requirements of all, but some schools and some teachers are sensitive to the breadth required and respond both through the structure of the school curriculum and its staffing, as well as by encouraging a variety of teaching methods that will stimulate the pupil. There is no question that this is not done in a very large number of schools.

Content and method

My approach has always been that content and the process of learning go hand in hand, each is important and each, if well planned, lends support to the other. However, close observation of pupils with learning difficulties has sown a seed of doubt which has not been resolved. The reason for the doubt is that most, but not all, of the successful teaching seen over the last five years was directly the result of good teaching methods and/or the charisma of the teacher. Well-prepared and constructed lessons caught the interest and pupils did not appear to be particularly concerned about the content. Indeed, it seemed that the *staff* were more concerned about content, for they could then be seen to be teaching something 'worthwhile', 'useful' or 'important'. This is not to deny the value of content, for in all subjects pupils have virtually no say in the content of the syllabus, but *one* of the ways of teaching such pupils was through carefully thinking about learning strategies. It may be that Colleges of Education and other institutions should think much more specifically about how they prepare their students for teaching RE and other subjects in a mixed ability classroom, and those required skills should be reflected in their own teaching methods.

Related to this is the necessity to have clear aims in teaching. One middle school used a system of team-teaching and was successful in coping with the slow learner because, while all pupils shared in the lead lesson, the teachers had a different set of objectives for the pupil with learning difficulties. To the observer this demonstrated a clarity of purpose not found in every classroom. Each pupil, regardless of ability, knew exactly what was required, instructions were clear, simple yet direct. Each lesson was constructed so that teachers and pupils knew exactly what to do and how to do it. It was this clarity of aim that worked with success in another middle school in a very formal situation (see Chapter 2). Religious Education can be a difficult subject to *teach*, but it is easier to *learn* if the teacher has sorted out his or her aims and objectives.

The teacher of RE must also, it seems, come to some clear conclusions about the nature of the subject. Many teachers see RE as dealing essentially with abstract concepts. If that is the case there is a strong argument for giving up teaching RE in schools, especially first, middle and special schools, because one will always be wrestling with the problem of how to assess the pupil's understanding. In most of the schools RE was generally considered to be 'concrete with abstract connections' although one school didn't wish, given the age of the pupils, to distinguish history, legend and myth. Most wished to base their approach on the phenomena of religion – what people used, what they wore, famous people, symbols – even though they recognised the abstractions that lay behind them. As in other areas of education it was a question of whether content should be taught, regardless of what is learned, because the content is important and 'true'. The majority of teachers involved appeared to represent a range of religious belief and non-belief. They were never asked about their commitment to any religion and most never volunteered the information.

Thus, as one might expect, the phenomenological approach was attractive because it dealt with concrete aspects of religion and didn't demand a faith commitment, though in one or two schools it did require an understanding of what a faith commitment might be. If the teacher or the school believes that, for example, the Bible is true and *must* be taught, then the problem of how one teaches a literary work to non-literate pupils becomes crucial. None of the schools in the project adopted this approach but elsewhere it has raised problems, for it carries with it the issue of meaning and correct interpretation. One teacher is reported to have said his slow learners 'can grasp the meaning of parables' (K. Hyde, *Religion and Slow Learners*, 1969). Perhaps this is more a comment on a slow learning teacher than a slow learning pupil!

A further question already touched on is how far some of the attitudes shared by religions can affect the teacher-pupil relationship. Religion has a grey area in that, with the humanist, the atheist and the agnostic, it shares a common set of values. The moral values within many religions could be and often are endorsed by society as a whole. Is the teacher of religion bound to reinforce those values in the relationship with the pupil in a way not obligatory for a French or maths teacher? Particularly for the slow learner, who may not grasp that one can teach *about* something without being committed to it, the values of a particular religion may only have meaning in the way the pupil sees his or her relationship with the teacher. This is a very difficult area but it must be reasonable to assume that all teachers have a concern for the slow learner and all teachers must seek to help that pupil create a self-identity which is of worth and value. It is easy to see that if the RE teacher teaches about great religious leaders and how they have cared for people, he or she becomes inextricably bound up, in the pupils' eyes, with those values. This is another subject to be considered, for any discussion of values has to be seen in the whole context of the school, its curriculum and its relationship with pupil, teachers and the local community.

The desire to transmit something urgently as *true* can often inhibit the variety of approaches one might take. One school in the project had a teacher on the staff (not one of the teachers used), who was a fundamentalist Christian. In her desire to ensure pupils were taught The Truth, she became almost physically violent and certainly psychologically violent in her attempts to turn the 7-to-8-year-olds she taught to her faith before they passed on to another teacher.

Many of these concerns will be taken up later when looking at specific examples of work and how the pupils responded. The implications raised will then be considered in an evaluation of how the curriculum may be restructured in order to accommodate the slow learner. As has already been said, this is an essentially pragmatic exercise and takes its starting place from what actually happens in the classroom, so theoretical conclusions will not be appropriate.

Use of resources

Much of the above is relevant to all subjects of the curriculum and not just Religious Education, but it appears that some of the most successful teaching of RE to pupils with learning difficulties has involved major changes in curriculum planning and teacher attitudes. Given that the RE teacher has won some or all of the battles above, what is the way forward? Again it is easy to sit on the sidelines but the following provide a sort of checklist which might be useful:

1 When reflecting on the appropriate content for a series of lessons, consider whether the pupil with learning difficulties can begin at the same point as everyone else. It seems to be the case that greater success

can be achieved if you stop thinking of how to water lessons down so the slow learner can grasp something. Instead you should plan a greater concentration in the lesson (a series of stage objectives in educational jargon) so that all pupils begin together, but move on according to ability, interest, etc. Initially this must involve more thought and more planning, but it can reduce workload in the classroom as each pupil should be clear where and how to progress to the next stage.

2   Think about trying a variety of teaching methods and try not to be worried if they don't succeed immediately. As teachers we learn in a variety of ways and so do our pupils – often learning by experience is harder than learning by rote or by reading. It does require confidence to change or experiment with a particular teaching style and it is often difficult for a teacher with a great deal of experience to change. Some do however, and with great success. The pupils may not respond to every method and strategy but at least one is continually probing to discover where the pupil's most effective response lies. Such changes may involve group work, use of role play and drama, visual aids and tape recorders. Bear in mind that one of the slow learner's problems is that of confidence and achievement – even though little RE may be learned the pupil may develop a skill in another area.

3   One undervalued resource in the secondary school is the use of posters. Pupils working in small groups with a couple of posters and a work card or some directed observation can gain a great deal through discussion or some other form of art work. Posters have an advantage over slides in that they do not involve great preparation. Many of them are simply inappropriate to use with a whole class as they are too small but in a group of 4 or 5 pupils they are excellent.

4   At the moment it is quite difficult to use videos effectively, many are too long and need to be stopped after every five minutes or so to re-view or discuss what has happened. This means that a half an hour video could take four or five lessons to look at properly and this can involve complicated booking arrangements. The slow learner has to be clear what to look for, what to note down and what the objectives are. This, in turn, means the teacher has had to watch the video, plan where to stop it and make it clear that the pupils should look for specific things. Again this is time-consuming in preparation, though one of the conclusions from this whole project is that good careful preparation benefits the pupil and the teacher.

Experiences of teachers using video will vary but my experience has been that pupils will not watch if the quality is poor, one scene is dwelt upon for too long or there is no definite action to catch the attention. Hence the importance of directed viewing for the slow learner. This was used with success in one of the middle schools using slides and there is no reason to suppose the same rules do not apply to videos.

5   It might be helpful to begin any new topic with an invitation to all the pupils to pool their knowledge either as a whole class or initially within groups. This can have a number of advantages:

(a)   it allows each pupil regardless of ability to say something about a particular topic

(b)   it enables the teacher to discover what the pupils already know, or wish to admit they know

(c)   it helps the teacher to remember that pupils acquire knowledge from a whole range of sources, not only the teacher

(d)   it is the common starting point upon which further work can be based

6   Finally though there are many more approaches, it can be helpful to admit ignorance on occasions. The myth of the teacher as all-knowing is convenient and useful but to confess ignorance from time to time at least gives the pupil with learning problems an ally from time to time. A willingness to admit ignorance and to find out the answers does not appear to be a weakness, it is an acknowledgement of one's humanity.

Is there an essential curriculum?

I wondered if this brief section should simply read 'no', but this is not quite true. One of the thrusts of this book is to advance the theory that content in RE has been overrated and one should look for a much closer link between the process of learning and what is to be taught. Personally, I feel this link appears much closer in special, primary and middle schools than in most secondary schools.

Content though is important. It is important because if RE is to remain on the curriculum it must be primarily concerned with religion. An RE syllabus that declines into moralistic situations and omits the very stuff of religion does a disservice to religion and, more important, the pupils. It would be hard to justify an RE syllabus in Britain as a whole which did not deal substantially with Christianity. Equally it would seem odd to ignore the other religions present, though for educational purposes it might be appropriate only to deal with one or two of them in any depth.

Pupils, it seems to me, have a very clear idea of what they consider religion to be and, while this view may not be shared by all teachers, it is important to respond somehow to this expectation. An example of how pupils' expectations do not always accord with reality happened in a school in Lancashire. The head teacher of fifteen years had never caned anyone, nor worn a gown or a mortarboard but pictures of 'Sir' sporting all three could be found chalked on walls from time to time. The influence of *The Beano* is stronger than one thinks. Similarly the impression of how religious people act and think acquired through TV and the press can affect pupils' ideas.

Should content be relevant? Surely relevance is relative. The only relevance is that what is taught is taught well, with good resources, and is about religion.

2

Teaching in the primary and middle school classroom

This chapter considers the work done in RE in four schools. There are three middle (deemed primary) schools and one primary school; two are rural, two are urban; two are Church of England aided schools, one is a local authority school and the fourth is a Church of England controlled school. The importance of the last of these classifications is that the LEA school and the controlled school follow the local authority agreed syllabus for RE, whereas the governors are responsible for RE in the aided schools.

It is quite important to emphasise that there is no judgement to be made about the quality of RE in each school. Inevitably the experience, expertise and involvement of staff varies, as do the children. The purpose of describing the type of work developed in RE is to help other teachers develop schemes in their own schools and also to make them aware of the pitfalls that can occur.

The age range of the pupils in this chapter is from 9 to 12 – the middle years of schooling. However, one lesson that began to emerge from work with the ability and age range 9 to 16 was that it is not good curriculum or content planning to water down material for the slow learner. It is far more effective to begin where one judges them to be, where they can make their most effective response, and build up work for the more able from that solid base.

Cobbett Middle School

Cobbett Middle School is a local authority school where the new Agreed Syllabus for Religious Education is based upon the Hampshire Syllabus.

The buildings are modern, the classrooms light and airy. The catchment area is largely rural and market town and the reading ages of the pupils are generally very high on entry. At the time of the project there was no teacher with specific responsibility for RE although the head teacher had a particular interest in the subject.

Compared with the other schools involved in this project the literacy of the pupils was remarkably high, though there was still a wide range of ability. Thus the definition of a 'slow learner' was measured by the average ability of the class, rather than by IQ or on a reading scale. This is a factor mentioned elsewhere in the book – that the point of view of what constitutes a slow learner will vary from teacher to pupil to parent. Pupils are keenly aware of how their ability at a certain subject or in a specific area of learning relates to their peers. In effect they form their own hierarchy, measuring achievement by how well they perform in relation to other pupils rather than by the standard required by the teacher.

A more serious view of the relative speeds of learning is involved here which can be best demonstrated by an anecdote. Some years ago while lecturing at a teacher training institution a student I was supervising on teaching practice came back to college to talk about her first day in the classroom. She said the class teacher had pointed out to her the pupils (a) with good reading ability, (b) with a rapidly developing concept of number and (c) those who were 'trouble'. Now it seemed to me, in my cosy room at college, that the student had already fixed in her mind how the pupils would behave and learn during the period of her teaching practice. Her expectations were firmly fixed and it would be very difficult for her to formulate her own opinions without being guided by the class teacher's comments.

This is a common problem which appears to have no obvious resolution. It can be mitigated to some extent by talking about pupil-teacher relationships and the way some pupils respond better with some teachers. It is also helpful to ask the student to be a participant observer and watch one or two children for a short time noting *everything* they do. Quite often, though not always, it becomes apparent that the 'troublesome' pupil is not necessarily more disruptive than anyone else, they simply adopt habits or have manners which are socially unacceptable to the teacher. This, of course, has consequent effects upon the effectiveness of the pupil's learning and the way in which the teacher approaches every aspect of the pupil's school life.

To return to Cobbett Middle School, the teaching of RE depended largely on the energy of the head teacher who had developed and taught a course on 'signs and symbols'. It was based on the 'Discovering an Approach' method of the Lancaster Primary RE Project, although the head teacher had expanded and developed the work in order to relate it to his own interests and expertise. In addition, he had begun to develop another scheme of work on the subject of 'Rules' (see page 29ff). As it stands the scheme appears to be more concerned with Moral Education than Religious Education but it should be emphasised that this was the beginning, the starting point for future development. A further theme being undertaken was that of 'Courage'.

Those teachers involved in RE were all enthusiastic but conscious that they were introducing a programme largely devised by the head teacher and, however much he encouraged modification and amendment, they tended to stay very close to his suggestions. Apart from the anxiety of amending the head teacher's scheme of work, there were other reasons why the original plan was largely not developed:

1 Teachers need to feel confident within their subject area and the non-specialist can be inhibited by lack of detailed knowledge. This should not be confused with practical teaching ability. One of the features of some of the RE lessons at the school was that they lacked the vitality of other lessons taught with flair and confidence by the same teacher. There was a real problem of knowledge, or lack of it, creating insecurity and a recourse to the resources provided by the head teacher.

2 The main resource for these classes was a duplicated 'book' written by the head teacher. There were few modern, attractive library books for the RE teacher to use, and though the pupils' 'books' encouraged them to find out and discover more there was little effective support available. Audio-visual resources too were limited. This is not intended to be a negative picture of RE in the school, it simply highlights the fact that resources were thin or out-of-date.

The two teachers involved devised activities which supplemented the written word, like drama and story-telling (the latter excellently done) as well as some individual research for homework. There was scope for the able pupil to develop and a minimum expectation of work to be completed. However, the teachers felt they were not at home with the subject although they were both obviously excellent teachers in other ways and in other subject areas.

Specific concern for slow learners was not apparent, although the variety of teaching strategies used did allow all pupils to share in what was taking place in the classroom. One important feature, however, was the policy to teach via *themes*. There is little evidence to support the often practised theory that by beginning with signs, such as level crossing signs, the pupil makes the transference to recognising the potent power of a symbol. Themes are attractive to teachers because they begin with the pupils' experience, being understood by able and less able alike. However, the power of the symbol in religion has a force of its own and it is not clear whether pupils have the conceptual awareness to appreciate this, and it is even less clear whether they can make the leap from signs to symbols. Teaching through themes demands a sophistication and understanding on the part of the teacher to ensure that learning takes place. The slow learner may well manage with the theme at a superficial level but understanding at depth is more difficult to assess.

There were five key issues in the teaching of RE in this school. None affected only the slow learner but all contributed to the situation in which the slow learner was taught:

1   The limited resources for RE meant that teachers who were not specialists had some difficulty in supplementing both their own knowledge and that of the pupils. This limited the possible variety of teaching strategies and effectively meant that the themes worked out by the head teacher became definitive, rather than a base from which each teacher could extend and develop. Pupils were not able to use the library to any great degree as the book resources in RE were poor. These factors resulted in a general move to the norm – the safe teaching which means that most pupils could cope with most of the work. This apparent criticism is not to be taken as such: all the teachers possessed admirable skills which they used to the full, but in the end they had to rely on them and were not supported by adequate resources.

2   The regularity of the teaching method and a certain lack of confidence did appear to help some of the slow learners. They learned the regular procedures, felt able to manage the fairly limited expectations of the non-specialist teachers and acquired a security which came to be reflected in the rising standard of their work. It was ironic that the pace and approach of the subject became the means by which the less able found security. This observation from Cobbett Middle School was supported by the style and method of teaching at the Abbey School to be discussed in the next section.

3   Themes such as 'Signs and Symbols' and 'Rules' do not of themselves help pupils to identify and engage with the study of religion. This is extremely important for, if the religious aspects of such themes are not brought out, religion becomes an amalgam of morals and rules. This, again, may or may not be more easily recognised by the slow learner. These two areas in particular reflect something of the inherent values of society and are, perhaps, more 'useful' in the ordering of life than the conceptual aspects of religious belief and practice.

4   The lack of cohesive planning and clear formulation of aims and objectives meant that the slow learner relied heavily upon the pupils' book placed before him or her. Progression in RE was marked by working through the book rather than in any other form of activity. The issue of aims and objectives will be returned to later, it is an extremely important aspect of getting to grips with teaching the slow learner.

5   The school had high standards and the slow learner had to struggle, but the RE teaching did not stretch out the ability range. The expectations of the subject became average so the gulf that might have separated the very able from the slow learner was narrowed considerably.

As an example, here is an outline based on the theme 'Rules' for use with 10-year-olds. Comments were invited from the staff.

1   *Opening*
        Groups to make plays about the school with no rules and what might happen.
        Stories entitled 'The school with no rules'.
2   Our own school rules
        Groups/individuals to list the rules under headings good/bad.
        Discussion on reasons why the rule is thought to be good/bad.
        Why was the rule made?
        Leaflet to be given out or re-written by children.
        Perhaps you think the rule is right, but you still grumble.
        Should you?
3   Rules at home – times to be in, meal times, shared duties – washing up, errands, standards of behaviour – courtesy to visitors, shut the door, switch off the light, clothes.

Are the rules different for boys and girls?
Should they be?
Perhaps you agree that the rules are right but you still grumble
and often do not obey them.

4   *Family from One End Street* (Puffin)
   (a)   Read (30 copies).
   (b)   What codes of behaviour are reflected?
   (c)   Which do you like/not like?

5   Rules in Society – to organise pursuit of a common purpose.
   (a)   Rules in the air – stacking etc.
   (b)   Rules on the road – what happens when people disobey them?
         Driving on the wrong side of the road. Seat belts? Yes or no to
         compulsion?
   (c)   Ask a policeman in to talk about rules.
   (d)   Rules from the past – schools
                           inns/hotels
                           employment rules

6   Rules for developing skills like craft, woodwork, cookery, science,
     sport, playing an instrument.

7   Rules help us to live with our fellows with understanding and pleasure.
   (a)   Manners – the oil that makes the world go round
         Write own leaflet, in groups, leaflet suitable for other children to
         receive.
   (b)   Rules protect the weak. How? A well ordered society is one in
         which the weak are looked after. One definition of a civilisation
         is a society which looks after its weakest members well.
   (c)   Desert island – you are wrecked on a desert island – make up your
         own rules for living. Work in groups.

8   Must rules always be obeyed?
         Hitler and rules about Jews.
         In our own country – are there any bad laws? Is it right to try to
         change them by force? What about our responsibility? If the law
         says, kill babies, must we obey it because it is the law? Even if a
         majority government has passed it?
         St. Paul said:

         'Let every soul be subject unto the higher powers. For there is no

power but of God: the powers that be are ordained of God.'
(Romans 13.1)

9 Codes for living
   (a) Hammurabi and other early codes.
   (b) Decalogue – what Jesus added. What the ten commandments
        mean. Thou shalt not steal or is it, thou shalt not be caught? Or is
        it OK to steal from the Inland Revenue or a large company, but
        not from individuals?
        Stealing from shops locally.
        Thou shalt not kill. Except in war?
   (c) Rules of other religions.

Clearly one could comment both on the general approach to RE in the
school and on this particular scheme. Personally, I think it provides a good
framework from which to begin staff development. In other words it is
not yet a scheme ready to be put into operation in the classroom. In fact
this was acknowledged by the head teacher, but the hierarchy within
schools can often make frank and open discussion of a head teacher's
scheme of work rather difficult. The theme 'Rules' is one which suggests
an integrated approach (implied in the scheme) rather than one solely
about religion. The confidence of the staff may have been increased if it
could be seen that the initial suggestion had far wider implications than the
RE lesson. Here is a true integrating topic out of which can come all sorts
of creative, science and number activities as well as religious education.

The Abbey School

The Abbey School is a Church of England aided middle school (9–13) in a
large city. The school buildings are on three floors and the room usually
available for RE was the middle room of a hall divided into three
classrooms. The school has strong links with local churches, local clergy
visit the school frequently and the Eucharist is a regular feature of school
worship. The Head of RE moved schools during the project and because
of this the work had to concentrate on the other three schools. As well as
being an RE specialist, she had previously had considerable experience as
a remedial teacher in a secondary school.

   The class on which the project centred was a first year class of 9-year-
olds just arrived from a variety of first schools. The time allocation for RE
was a double period per week totalling 70 minutes. The work for the year

centred first on the Eucharist, then on the Gospel writers as pupils were in houses named after them and St. Alban, the patron saint of the school.

During the project the school was developing its own school Eucharist assisted by local clergy and others. It is necessary to appreciate this to understand why the first RE lesson the pupils received was from a local clergyman and on the Eucharist. The timetabling meant that, while the class had a reasonable amount of time allocated to RE, there was little continuity from week to week particularly with children more used to a first school type of timetable.

The academic level of the class was not formally tested but there were a number of pupils who had considerable difficulty in writing or drawing. The pupils were not set or streamed but the general standard of the class appeared quite low in relation to other classes of 9-year-olds visited in the city.

One of the most interesting features of the RE curriculum was that the Head of RE had very clear views on the most effective way of helping pupils (a) to understand religious beliefs and practices and (b) to develop skills of expression, both literary and artistic. In her experience, the most effective method of teaching new entrants to the school was to adopt a fairly traditional syllabus of content and an 'old-fashioned' teaching method. Both of these approaches were modified as the pupils progressed through the school but this was to be the beginning. It is not the purpose of this project to argue for or against a particular teaching style, but rather to note its effectiveness with the slow learner. As none of the other schools involved adopted such an approach, the Abbey School made a very useful contribution indeed.

Themes explored

Eucharist

The clergyman who first spoke to the pupils was pleasant and tried to establish good relationships with them. He talked for over an hour while showing some of the artefacts used, his cassock and surplice. The purpose of beginning with this topic was that the school would soon have its own Eucharist and it was felt the pupils should understand something of its importance and significance. In the subsequent weeks the teacher developed the theme of the Eucharist through the symbols of bread and wine. Bread was baked at home and taken into the classroom so that the pupils could share a piece of it together. During each lesson the pattern of work was largely the same: the teacher would impart some information, encourage the pupils to think about it and discuss it briefly, then write sentences on the board to be copied down and a picture, or series of pictures, to be drawn. This method was used throughout and the pupils rapidly became used to the established formula. Occasionally a worksheet was given out to be copied out with correct words put in spaces, but progress was very slow as many pupils had problems with reading and needed constant repetition of instructions. Here is an example of a worksheet on the Eucharist:

The Holy Communion Service

The Holy Communion Service is sometimes called the
_____ and sometimes the Eucharist which means
_____. We follow the actions of Jesus at the Last
_____. This meal was held in the upper _____ on the
night _____ Jesus died. He took the bread and gave it to
the disciples saying, 'This is my _____.' Then he took the
cup of _____ saying, 'This is my blood.' He shared it with
the _____. He asked his followers to go on doing this in
_____ of him. Today the priest puts the bread or wafers on a
_____ and the wine is put in a _____. He wears
special clothes like a cassock, an alb or surplice and a _____
or cloth which is a sign that the priest is a servant of God's people.
We had our first Eucharist at Abbey last _____.

before	paten	Thursday	wine	Mass
stole	disciples	room	chalice	Supper
remembrance	body	thanksgiving		

Now draw the chalice and paten that we use in
school on your plain page.

It must be remembered that the very formal, tightly-structured teaching was a deliberate policy by the teacher. The information given about the Gospel writers was terse and brief and not always reflective of contemporary thinking. This caused me problems when I was invited to teach two lessons, the first on St. Alban.

St. Alban

St. Alban is the patron saint of the school. Did the school want to enter into questions about his historical veracity and if and when he lived, or did they want the general story, found in many lives of saints, to be taught to the class? In fact the Head of RE didn't mind but in the classroom the pupils dictated the approach because they had come to expect clear statements written on the board and to be copied into the books. The lesson taught was a remarkable failure and it is worth recording in more detail.

The object was to encourage the pupils to respond to certain information. A pupil came to the front and the class was told he had committed a crime. What could it be? More pupils were brought out to guard the unfortunate prisoner. Did that give any more clues about the crime? The others, they were told next, were Roman soldiers . . . and the process went on until I hoped a picture of St. Alban and his 'crime' would have been built up by the class and questions about the historicity of the story would be seen in a different and less significant perspective. The lesson failed because of a number of reasons. Some of the more obvious are:

1   The classroom, inadequately divided, had to cope with noise from two adjacent classrooms and my own pupils had, equally, to be very careful of the noise they made themselves.

2   Having enjoyed the 'guessing game' most of the pupils looked to the blackboard in order to write down sentences and draw the picture. They were largely unable to make notes of their own volition.

3   I had not expected the pupils would be so rooted in the security of their own lessons plans and modes of learning. While I had engaged the pupils in an enjoyable activity they were not able to see what they had learned because it did not conform to the method normally used by the teacher.

4   The book which the school used with these pupils reinforced the teaching model of the teacher, so with her using the book on previous and subsequent occasions the pupils' learning patterns could not be realigned in one lesson, or even in several.

5   My own planning had not made sufficient allowance for the above and instead of developing the lesson by means of staged objectives I had plunged into the deep end and felt myself drowning!

St. Luke

The second lesson was to be on St. Luke. Here again the questions raised in my own mind were considered largely irrelevant to the pupils: should one be honest with them and say there is really very little indeed known about him even to the extent of some modern researchers doubting he accompanied St. Paul on part of his journey and that he wasn't a doctor as tradition suggests? Or should one stick to the tried and tested formula where legendary figures are given the benefit of historical doubt? It was a difficult decision especially as other lessons about parallel figures had taken the latter course. To use the expected formula fitted in with the pupils' expected mode of learning and was simply more convenient when the usual lessons took a straightforward 'copy off the blackboard and draw the picture' form.

Given the experience of the lesson on St. Alban it was clear to me that given one lesson, the pupils' expectations, the classroom and the approach of the textbook, I should simply follow the pattern of the normal lesson. This was, in itself, an interesting experience because I felt that I was 'selling myself' by endorsing an approach and a form of content with which I profoundly disagreed. It was also easier – a not insignificant factor. There was no noise and the pupils knew what was expected but it seemed to me that I was reinforcing the wrong approach and certainly was giving them doubtful information.

Teaching style

It is as well to reiterate here that this teaching style was a deliberate policy on the part of the teacher and it is important in the context of this project to consider some of the reasons for it:

1   It has been, and largely remains, a popular concept in Religious Education since the 1960s that pupils should not be taught anything they have to 'unlearn' later. Yet in many other subjects pupils unlearn and certainly most adults would acknowledge that experience and age has caused them to unlearn many things taught to them in school. If one has some sympathy with this then content becomes less important. It will be forgotten or amended as the pupil grows through school

and on into adulthood. What is important is the acquisition of skills that makes unlearning possible, relatively painless and 'normal'.

2   For pupils just arrived from a variety of schools it is important to create a security not only in the pastoral sense, but in learning style. If one adds to this the generally low ability of pupils then it becomes extremely important to give them practice in the skills which they will need, like writing, reading and taking care over their work. The regularity of each lesson, its solid structure, and emphasis on reading the words on the board before carefully copying them into their books enables pupils to acquire that security.

3   One fact did come to light during the Project and made a considerable impact. Halfway through that first school year one could see a marked improvement in hand-writing, neater books and enthusiasm on the part of many pupils to demonstrate that improvement. Whether they had developed any deeper insight into religion was not clear but, as the teacher remarked, many of the less able had acquired a platform from which they could spring off into other areas. As they proceeded through the school, drama, creative writing, role play and so on would unfold before them in their RE lessons and they could respond more effectively because of that discipline learned in that first year. One may have doubts about how easy it would be to develop new learning styles, but one cannot dismiss the theory in RE that *learning for now* is important. It gives the pupil new experiences that they will not need to 'unlearn' but 're-learn' later.

This experience at Abbey School raised a number of aspects very pertinent to RE as well as to the slow learner. These questions will be considered again later (see Chapter 4).

1   Should the content of RE be a secondary consideration in relation to the skills required by less able pupils?

2   Is the need for a secure, stereotyped pattern of learning necessary for the less able and, if so, how does that affect the nature of RE taught?

3   How much can the pupils' interest and commitment to a subject and/or a teacher be related to their own assessment of their progress?

4   Is it possible that the careful development syllabuses of the last ten to fifteen years are irrelevant, because the mode or method of learning is far more important than content as far as the less able pupil is concerned?

Wenbury School

Wenbury Middle School is a controlled school in a rural situation drawing on a wide catchment area. The buildings are fairly new and it has a good library. The head teacher is particularly interested in the integration of children with physical or other handicaps into the school. The Head of RE in the school also has responsibility for Remedial Education so there is a natural and established link between the two subjects. The support for RE in the school is excellent, the department being well resourced with books, slides, tapes and artefacts. The project lasted for two years. A third year class was followed into the fourth year and another third year class was observed.

The method of teaching adopted was team-teaching. The Head of RE worked with another member of staff on each occasion and the success of the first year's experiment encouraged her to repeat the experience with another teacher. So she team-taught with a colleague for two years and in the second year linked with a colleague in another class. The general pattern of team-teaching was for one or other of the teachers to take a lead lesson. The time allocated for RE was a double period and the stimulus normally lasted for 20 to 30 minutes. Two classes were in the same large room and they remained together as a large group for the whole time. Each class was designated to one of the two teachers who marked homework and so on, but there was a freedom of movement on the part of the teachers during the class period. During the stimulus, or lead lesson, the pupils would be encouraged to make their own notes on what was said or seen. These would be used in the follow-up lessons. There was never any dictation.

The RE Syllabus for the County Authority is based on the Hampshire Syllabus, though it was not formally adopted until the middle of the two year period. It made little difference to the school syllabus as the teaching was already in general agreement with the aims and objectives of the new Agreed Syllabus. The approach was to take themes across religions like festivals, sacred writings and marriage. The aim of this thematic approach was not to give every religion equal treatment but to enable the pupils to recognise the importance of the variety of religious traditions and particularly of the major religion in Britain, Christianity.

The object of the project was not to analyse either team-teaching per se or how one teaches world religions in a rural area, though this school would provide interesting illustrations for both aspects. The aim was to see how team-teaching could help the slow learner in RE. There are four points of relevance to the project which should be borne in mind.

1   The school policy was that each subject should be examined regularly, however some staff were opposed to RE being an examination subject. Their view was that one could not assess a pupil's religious awareness, one could not apply the same criteria to it as to other subjects, so it should not be examined. This view would appear to represent a misunderstanding of the aim of the RE in the school and in many others. The eventual conclusion was that RE would be examined in the same way as other subjects but the issue of examinations will be raised later (see Chapter 4).

2   It is worth noting the first lesson seen in the school which was untypical of what was to follow. It is referred to not in criticism but because later work was so stimulating and lively. This was prior to any team-teaching and the teacher, with several pupils with learning difficulties in a large class, was trying to cope with the different demands of the pupils. They read a story from a book, answered the questions and then, if there was time, drew a picture. The slow learners read aloud to her while the others worked and then traced the picture. It is important to recognise that with a class of nearly thirty, with six or so very poor readers, the teacher was in the quandary of how to cope with a diversity of demands and yet not be able to prepare a variety of activities because of the time available to her.

3   While the Head of RE was a specialist the two other teachers were not, though one particularly was interested in RE. Because of the team-teaching situation the Head of RE was able (a) to encourage more staff to participate with her guidance and support as a specialist and (b) to open up the subject to scrutiny and comment from the staff as a whole. In other words she brought RE out of a position where it revolved around her and enabled other staff not only to participate but to take the initiative. This approach had a direct effect on the staff teaching RE, helping to increase their confidence, and also on the pupils, as they recognised their 'shared learning'.

4   Religion was seen to be important within the school. There were attractive displays put up in the corridors and classrooms, school worship was taken seriously, though it was not always necessarily serious, local clergy visited the school. All this helped the teachers to present the subject to the pupils as worthwhile. They had the opportunity to recognize the importance of religion for some people, though they may have no religion themselves.

Method

The idea of the stimulus session meant that each teacher would take it in turns to prepare the week's double lesson. Clearly the Head of RE helped her colleague with available resources but the alternating of teachers meant that the whole group of over 50 pupils had a different style and different approach from week to week. This made a nice balance from the informative to the flamboyant and the lessons observed were vigorous and full of vitality. The support of a colleague also helped the pupils to recognise that the teacher did not 'know' everything and questions to the colleague helped them to recognise the fragility of knowledge as well as encouraging them not to be afraid to ask questions.

Early in the project the Head of Department noted that after a stimulus some of the poor readers were not completing their worksheets and they had not paid much attention during the stimulus. She surmised, and experience appeared to prove her correct, that it was because some of the slow learners were not clear how the stimulus would help them with their work. If they were inattentive when the time came to read and write the teacher would help by repeating what had already been said. This problem, of course, is not new nor is it easily cured but, during the project, the teacher was careful at the beginning of each lesson to outline its relevance to previous work as well as what would be expected during the next 80 minutes or so and generally made the objectives and context of the lesson very clear. This helped everyone, but particularly the slow learners who certainly appeared to gain in confidence and attentiveness over the weeks.

The Head of Department and the other staff involved believed in a variety of activities in the classroom. Thus while a stimulus might be slides one week, it could be a talk or artefacts on another occasion. On some occasions the classroom was set out with a variety of materials and the pupils were encouraged to find out for themselves from the information available. This did not *only* help the slow learners because it offered a variety of learning modes, but raised the general level of interest and enthusiasm of the class. The slow learners were not trapped in a system of teaching/learning which did not work for them. In fact the variety of activity within each lesson meant that those who had a limited attention span were able to turn their minds to different tasks within the period.

Two examples of worksheets are given here relating to festivals of light. The class would have received a stimulus and then most of them would be given the sheet to complete. Both teachers were thus available to move freely around the class helping and encouraging the pupils.

Hanukah

Copy and complete:

Hanukah is a festival of _____ celebrated by the

_____. It means _____. Hanukah lasts for

_____ days and commemorates the time when Judas

_____ forced the _____ out of the temple in

_____. The Jews used light to _____ the temple and

the story is that the only lamp of _____ that could be found

burnt for eight _____.

Using the materials in the room, complete the following tasks and record your answers. Do each section, but start with any one.

Hanukah Food

Why is the food fried? Make a list of traditional Hanukah food. Try a piece of latke. What is latke made of?

The Dreidel

Draw a dreidel. Explain what it stands for. How is it used? Why was it a good idea when the Jews were being persecuted?

The Chanukiyah

What is it? Why are there nine candles? What is the centre one called? Read and write out a prayer associated with the lighting of one of the candles. Design a chanukiyah of your own.

Diwali

Copy and complete:

Diwali is a festival of _____ and is celebrated by the

H_____, Sikhs and B_____. The story is told of

_____ who was exiled to the forest with his wife

_____. Sita was kidnapped by _____, the demon

king. He took Sita to _____ to get his revenge on Rama

who was _____, kind and gentle. After a bitter struggle,

Rama slays _____ and returns home with Sita. his people

were so pleased that they put lights on every building as a sign of

_____, and to drive away all the powers of _____.

How is the festival celebrated today?

Either:
Find pictures of Rama, Sita and Ravana and draw them in your book.

Or:
Draw and colour a picture of people celebrating Diwali today.

Homework

Think of being trapped in the dark. How would you feel?
Someone with a light finds you. What would you think about them?
Write a poem or short story called 'Trapped in the dark'.

The slow learners' activities varied from being given a sheet and a regular visit from one of the two teachers to one or two pupils being given a sentence cut up into individual words to arrange in the correct order. One pupil particularly used this method instead of inserting the missing word and before going on to do the later exercises. This reflected a compromise between giving them either work totally different from the rest of the class or a worksheet they were unable to complete. Did it work? The question of assessment will come later but certainly by the end of the project all pupils were working from the worksheets.

Were themes helpful? Again it depends upon which model of assessment one chooses because literate pupils will nearly always achieve more in written examinations than their peers. They were helpful in that pupils were able to recognise the familiar themes which recur in religion and to understand that what people wear, what they eat, their festivals, marriage ceremonies and rites of passage are important. A pattern of 'religious' behaviour and practice may be built up, or at least assimilated in some way. Themes are colourful and essentially practical, they are based upon what people do and where they go, the philosophy of religious studies may come later but in these themes one is encountering concrete examples.

Assessment

The Head of RE, having been a party to the debate on examinations, was concerned that *all* the pupils should be examined but the problem of examining the slow learner was a real one. She experimented with a form of examination that didn't just require a written paper but included overhead projectors and a cassette recorder. Thus the slow learner would still be handicapped to some degree by lack of literacy but there would be questions and answers that did not require literacy of a high degree .

It is not possible to give a sample of the examination because it was conducted in the form of a festival itself. Multiple choice questions were asked, candles were lit, pupils were invited to say if they had enjoyed their work on festivals or not and why, food was shared and the session ended with a look forward to next term. In other words the examination on the term's work on festivals was imaginatively constructed around the idea of a festival to include the asking of questions. Here again the slow learner may not have excelled but the situation in which the examination took place was not as threatening, it was conducted in the context of a term's work and there were questions which could be answered by all as well as questions demanding more detailed response.

The previous year one of the pupils with a poor reading age had done quite well in the examination, obtaining a 'C' grade (average). Some staff were opposed to giving the grade because it would make the parents think their child was 'brighter' than they had been led to believe. This raised problems about examinations and assessment. The view of some of the staff appeared to be that examinations should fulfil the teacher's expectations of the pupil and nothing must happen to upset that expectation. The RE teacher argued that if examinations are to mean anything (and remember this is a middle school) then the responsibility is on the examiner to devise ways and means of enabling a pupil to express what she or he knows. The pupil who had done quite well obviously 'knew' more than he was able to express through the written language but had to cope with a handicap – poor reading and writing – that didn't allow him to express what was within. The teacher argued that this is a handicap in itself to which all teachers must address themselves and not just RE teachers.

The teachers at this school had gone out of their way to teach RE in a pleasant room, with good resources, using an interesting and engaging method. This was not designed for the slow learner but it all contributed to the general enthusiasm for the subject. This seemed, subjectively, to be a vital part of the assessment of the programme, pupils (generally) enjoyed the lessons, there was an air of interest and fun, and the enthusiasm was infectious. There were no behaviour problems and the high standard of teaching carried the slow learner along on the tide.

Conclusions

1 Content may not matter if one's prime aim is to raise the general level of literacy. However, in this school the prime aim was to develop the pupils' awareness of and sensitivity to religion, so content did matter. This may be partly due to the teachers' understanding of religion and its importance in enabling the pupil to understand the world in which she or he lives. The resources used supported this idea, they were varied, stimulating and modern, not limited to one book or one style of teaching.

2 The pupils were clearly told what to do, how to do it, where to look for further information, how a particular resource or stimulus would help and how what they were doing fitted into the overall pattern of work expected of them.

3 The variety of teaching methods not available to one teacher but to

two in a team made for a greater flexibility and interest in the classroom. The Head of RE and her two colleagues found it rewarding and, with a willingness to support rather than criticise each other, the atmosphere in the classroom was relaxed and stimulating.

4   The commitment to the slow learner was not just made in teaching methods but also through curriculum strategy. The timetabling of staff and the willingness to approach RE through pupil participation rather than teacher instruction opened up a variety of options.

5   The question of assessment vis-à-vis examinations is a difficult one but it is helpful if teachers can be sure of their objectives and pupils can see precisely what is required.

St. Joseph's School

St. Joseph's School is a Church of England aided primary school in London. The pupils are of mixed religious backgrounds including a number of West Indian Pentecostals, Muslims and Hindus although most of the children appeared to have no particular religion. It is housed in modern buildings about 300 metres away from the parish church. The head teacher and the two class teachers involved with the project were extremely supportive during the two years.

The approach in this school was different from that in the other three schools. Virtually all the teaching in the project was carried out by myself with the staff helping and assisting with on-going work. The method was a useful complement to the type of work being carried out elsewhere, but it did present certain drawbacks which will be mentioned later. It also required a heavy commitment of time. Instead of monitoring the work of other teachers I spent a considerable amount of time in school and gained a closer insight into the work. Over the two years there were two groups of pupils and the activities engaged in will be described sequentially. The age range was different: year one was made up of 10–11-year-olds and year two of 9–10-year-olds.

Year one activities

Of the ten children in the top class (six girls, four boys) there was a wide range in their ability to read and write with any degree of fluency. Most noticeable however, particularly among the boys, was a lack of confidence both to produce worthwhile work and in themselves as people. The other feature of the group that remained very much in evidence during the year was the sex division. It was extremely difficult to set two groups working that divided on anything other than a sex basis. My hunch is that this was more related to the issue of confidence than to anything in the school, which seemed to go out of its way to treat pupils equally.

The local church

The whole class visited the local parish church for a conducted tour which was, in effect, a history tour – interesting but geared to the more able, for a lot of information was imparted in a short time. The following week the slow learner group returned and two activities were begun.

1   The children sat in the pews and were asked to think of words which might describe their feelings in the church: 'dark', 'smelly', 'damp', 'bird droppings all over the place' were some of the comments. A list of about 10 to 15 words was obtained. The children stood in the (quite high) pulpit and were asked what it felt like. Again their list of words was noted, for example 'embarrassing'.

　　On returning to the classroom the list was put up on the board and memories refreshed about how the words had come from feelings in the church. Pupils were then asked to write a short poem or sentence using some of the words they had suggested. They quite liked this, and although the very poor writers copied words from the board they were selective in their choice. While the quality of sentence or poem varied, all the pupils had thought about their feelings in the church and collected together a short series of words that expressed those feelings.

2   The church had a number of stained glass windows. The pupils looked at them carefully noting the colours, the dominant colours and the overall impression. In the classroom they were asked to design a pattern for a window and then, using coloured tissue paper, to create their own window. This was a new activity for them. Some found it extremely hard to think of a pattern and transmit it to the paper, others could do that but found equal difficulty in using coloured paper to create an effect. There was no doubt that while they were willing and one or two produced very effective designs the overall task of relating a vision in the mind to paper and then using necessary manipulative skills caused problems for most of them. It was not a disaster but they were disappointed with the results.

Of these two activities the former was perhaps the most successful; it encouraged the pupils to explore their personal experiences and they could listen to other pupils' feelings in the church. The writing was an effort but most tried very hard. The second activity was not only difficult, but it highlighted one of the real problems of the slow learner. When the windows were completed they were displayed on the classroom window. There was an ambivalence on the part of most children because, while they liked seeing their work on display, it was plain to them and others that it was nowhere near the general level of other work displayed in the classroom. So their pride of achievement was counterbalanced by the reinforcement of their inadequacy in relation to other pupils. This must be a real and difficult problem for all teachers – how to balance achievement with reinforcement of inadequacy.

The film

This experience in the first few weeks led to the idea that what the pupils did should not be seen to be in competition with any other activity in the very creative school environment. Back in the church again one pupil announced that the place was so damp and creepy it should be pulled down. Another pupil who didn't attend the church said that it would be awful to do that, so inevitably an argument (not a debate) developed about whether the church should be knocked down to be replaced by a cinema, bingo hall or supermarket – or not. Some pupils apparently liked having a church nearby.

It was decided to make a film to illustrate the problem. The school had a Super 8 camera and the soundtrack could be added later on a cassette. Pupils were asked to think about the story. This was a very difficult exercise for them as they tended to think in grandiose, epic-like, terms rather than to consider practically how they could cope with materials available. However, they were left with the teacher and a tape-recorder for a week to think over a storyboard.

On returning the sex split had happened. The girls wanted to do the church film but the boys wanted to make a film about Christmas. The obvious solution to the impasse was to make two films – so they did.

Christmas

One of the boys, Richard, thought up a basic story on tape with the other boys chiming in. They created a storyboard with drawings of what each major shot should be concerned with. All pupils handled the camera and learned how to operate it. Each of them was to have a part in the film and shoot some of the footage. The preparation for a three minute film was lengthy with credits and titles having to be made, props obtained from various parts of the school, a chimney made with snow on and things brought from home. Again and again they discussed how the story would unfold and how they would distribute parts.

The pupils shot *all* the footage and decided on the camera angles but there was only one rule. In order to help them appreciate how films are made, it was not shot in sequence for it was intended they should each learn how to cut and splice. There were two major problems. Firstly, the lights in the school were not really strong enough to give a good light for the indoor shots and secondly the splicing equipment from the Teachers' Centre had parts missing so they couldn't do that themselves.

The soundtrack was made after splicing and the pupils sang some songs as a background to events on the film. It was a very useful practice exercise but they were rather disappointed with the result when the film first came back from printing because, of course, it was not in sequence nor was there a soundtrack.

Burning the church

Again much of the activity was repeated except they were now all much more expert, needed very little help and began to assert themselves in roles. One was very good at thinking out new camera angles, another became the acknowledged 'expert' on the equipment, others took over the props. Most of this film was shot outside the school. They were more prepared for the first viewing of the film and produced an excellent soundtrack to accompany it. At the end of this film most felt able to make their own film, they certainly knew how to handle simple film equipment and one or two had given expression to a creative talent in developing stories and stage direction.

The church was actually destroyed in the film by accident – the model burned down and the film ended with arguments about whether it should be rebuilt.

Where does this fit into Religious Education? The film 'Christmas' was about receiving presents and this is how many children conceive Christmas, especially if they come from non–Christian homes. There is obvious goodwill in giving and receiving gifts but this need not be part of the

Christmas message. For the pupils the process of film-making was more important than the content.

The head teacher of the school noted how the boys particularly appeared to develop much more self-confidence during these two terms of project work, they became more forthcoming and more willing to participate in the general life of the school. Those who see a close relationship between religion and personal development may be encouraged to see a link here but it is a tenuous link. Certainly all the pupils gained in confidence because, whatever the inadequacies of each film (and the second was quite good), they were doing something no other group had done in the school and others rather envied the opportunity open to them. They were not in competition but rather in a situation where they were envied and admired.

The issues surrounding the films did evoke some discussion about the usefulness of a church and its importance to a local community as well as the importance of Christmas as a festival. During the film, for the sake of a story, they thought of reasons for and against the existence of the church, what type of people would want to keep it going etc. So in a real sense they did look at the role of religion in a local community, though whether they would have identified it as RE is another matter.

The words of 'feeling' developed out of sitting in the church were also valuable though again it would not be readily identified by the pupils as having anything to do with RE. The exercise is important, however, because one of the issues one returns to again and again with the slow learner is that while they can, and do, become enthusiastic, have good ideas and generally want to participate, they can have problems expressing the reasons for their enthusiasm as they lack the verbal fluency so important in contemporary British society. In turn this leads to frustration and then lack of enthusiasm as nothing kills enthusiasm like someone else's lack of understanding and lack of response.

Year two activities

This group of children represented a much wider ability range. Of the six pupils one was very able but disruptive, one was of about average ability for her age, one was extremely poorly motivated and the others represented varying degrees of literacy.

The Hebrew alphabet

Initially it seemed reasonable to assume that the pupils should engage in something very different from the other group to avoid the issue of competition. Also it was decided that the project should attempt to do something about the literacy of the pupils, resistant as they were to reading and books.

The approach was to bring in a Hebrew Bible so that they would be able to see the language of the scriptures (the Christian Old Testament). This was supported by a very large A4 photograph of four or five verses so the form of the letters could be clearly seen. Some discussion took place about the language running from right to left rather than left to right and the vowels being represented in the text by the pointing, using dots and dashes below and above the letters. The aim was to show language as a code, a system of symbols which could be learned, but to approach it through a language other than English.

The pupils wrote words without vowels, separating out words in simple sentences and wrote their names in a transliteration of Hebrew letters. It was not a very successful exercise, though two of the pupils became quite interested and continued the work at home over a couple of weeks. The novelty wore off, however, without any real indication that they were able to recognise the nature of the language code.

Visit to Chichester Cathedral

During a week's visit to Chichester the pupils, together with the rest of their class, visited the Cathedral and spent about an hour and a half there altogether. Over the week they also visited a nature conservancy area, the seaside, Portsmouth harbour and the market – a variety of experiences. Ten days after their return to school I asked members of the group individually what they could remember most clearly of their visit. Three of them mentioned the Cathedral and all independently commented on the size of the building and the amount of space inside. As a group they remembered very little of the contents, the awareness of space was the most common feature. It may be that the value of such visits is not the information passed to children but their feelings and emotions within the space – those need to be probed and encouraged.

Christmas activities

As Christmas drew near it became clear that regardless of each pupil's religious or non-religious view, there was a sense of excitement and anticipation. During one conversation it was agreed to write letters to various people asking them how they spent Christmas. This was not an easy activity because of the writing problem, however all the pupils were motivated to write at least two letters to people of their choice including Princess Diana, Bob Paisley, then manager of Liverpool FC, Martin Shaw, an actor, the presenters of the TV programme 'Game for a Laugh', Ernie Wise and the late Eric Morecombe. All wrote letters and most received replies. The pupils were able to see how some other people spent their Christmas holiday and, though it was disappointing that some did not reply, the group did have quite a collection of how various people, famous and not so famous, celebrated Christmas. It also highlighted how some saw it principally as a religious festival while others considered it a break from the daily round of activities.

Hats

In conversation one of the pupils began to refer to 'paki hats' and it transpired that he was referring to turbans. This continued reference annoyed a Pakistani girl in the group. It was, of course, not only rude but ill-informed. A small project on 'hats' was begun in order to see what a great variety of hats there was and how the wearing of a hat may be useful as well as define a role. The children worked with enthusiasm; they used the library, drew hats, talked about them, noted how some people wore different sorts of hats – police officers, firefighters, priests, bishops, people in hot countries, cold countries and so on.

The success of this activity was varied. Certainly most of the children were enthusiastic and worked extremely well. The activity lasted for some time and each pupil was able to see how, just as they might wear special clothes on special occasions, so priests and other religious leaders often wore special clothes to signify their position. The balloon of success was punctured by the original comment, repeated after spending a long time on the activity. Clearly learning about hats didn't undermine the offensive name for turbans. Prejudice is not necessarily dispelled by knowledge, it is far more deep-rooted than that. The pupil in question couldn't see why the term should be offensive nor did he feel it should affect his generally good relationship with the Pakistani girl in question.

The Tower of London

This small group was taken on two day visits. Each of the three pairs was given a cassette recorder and a blank cassette in order to record the sounds of their trip and any comments they felt able to make as they went on their journey. The first day visit was to the Tower of London, the second was to the Science Museum. There were a number of purposes for these visits:

(a) to help them become aware of the sounds that exist around them
(b) to see how they would react in a different environment from the school
(c) to see what they would remember and develop upon back in the classroom
(d) to see how helpful a cassette could be if used in place of workcards etc.

The Tower offered a cultural setting with a strong historical tradition and the crown jewels offered a unique insight into pageantry and the manner in which they are displayed can make them the subject of some degree of wonder.

The details of the visit are not particularly important except for one or two incidents. One boy, of Turkish origin, was amazed to discover Turkish cannon in the Tower and from then on he displayed an almost proprietorial air about the place – an interesting indication of how a young boy will look back to his origins or, more correctly, his parents' origins. A visit to a very *British* place became more alive because of the Turkish element.

The chapel in the White Tower was not identified as a chapel or as having any significance at all, religious or otherwise. When asked about the chapel, one of the pupils said that all the other rooms had lots of things in like armour and weapons but 'that room' was empty. One cannot make generalisations from this but that particular pupil was one of those who commented on the space in Chichester Cathedral. One wonders how society does transmit its values to the young, in this case a sense of silence and peace, although children were bound up in the world of speed and immediate visual and aural response. (Clearly more work could be done here and the work of the Religious Experience Unit at Manchester College, Oxford may throw some light on these experiences and how they may be interpreted.)

The last particular item of interest was the visit to the crown jewels. Understandably the pupils did not know what many of the items were. They did recognise the crowns, but not the significance of any crosses on them. Most remarkably, in spite of only one child having seen them previously, they were not very interested in them. A slow walk around them can be followed by a longer look from a little further away, but none of them really wanted to look for much longer. Perhaps one brings adult values to the child's world? One or two children were keen to record things on their tape, not because of the jewels, but because they had been asked to and because they liked playing and replaying their tapes. At lunch I asked them as a group for any feelings they had about the visit to the jewels, but it was clear that the door on the way in, like a huge safe door, was a greater attraction than the jewels themselves. Again this is a complex area involving expectation, attitudes and the way in which children assimilate ideas and values from society.

On their return to the school the pupils listened to the tapes again and were encouraged to respond to the visit in any way they wished. The most remarkable piece of work was by the pupil with the greatest problems with reading and writing – a carefully composed and detailed picture of the Tower with a Beefeater outside. Clearly the effort was tremendous, in many ways it was his best piece of work for the year, yet during the visit itself he had appeared listless and uninterested. There needs to be more research in education and especially in Religious Education on how the teacher presents an issue to the pupil and how the pupil recognises what response can be made.

The Science Museum

The Science Museum visit was also recorded and the response of the children was similar to that of the first visit. Both visits illustrated the difficulties of expressing enthusiasm and the very brief attention span – some pupils asked very perceptive questions but could not wait for an answer, even if one could be given. Immediacy appeared to be crucial in responding to the world, which may have been the reason for ignoring the chapel in the Tower visit. Was this to do with the pace of life, with a belief that questions are not to be answered, or if they are, that the answer is likely to be too complex or too abstract?

The hidden value of such visits was that the children recognised that they were important, they were 'special' in the sense that they were doing something envied by the rest of the class. While the visit as such may or may not have deepened their education, it did give them a recognition of their own worth. In the classroom they demonstrated their inadequacy and 'worthlessness' all the time. The time spent with them was an invaluable part of the project, for it was as their confidence grew that I was more able to appreciate some of their inhibitions about learning. It was interesting to see how these inhibitions related to how much they liked the school or the teachers, to parental pressures and the ability of brothers or sisters – factors which indicate the complexity of sorting out the problems facing a child deemed slow learner.

Bible stories

The telling of stories has been the most popular way of handing on a society's and a religion's values. The religious 'myth' should never be underestimated. One common complaint of teachers is that children seem to be unable to remember the meaning of the story. The slow-learning child has an even greater problem remembering not only the story but the meaning as well. But who is it that knows the meaning of any story? The layers of meaning that exist in the stories in the Jewish and Christian traditions have provided scholarship with the tools of theological, sociological, historical and linguistic reflection, but it is still a brave or foolhardy person who can claim to know *the* meaning.

The purpose of this exercise was to tell or re-tell a well-known Bible story to the children and then try to help them explore their own reactions to the story. Not all pupils were from the Christian tradition but in the church school some stories would be familiar. There were three stories: the Parable of the Good Samaritan, the Prodigal Son, and the Nativity. Only one example is included here because we are more concerned with the approach than the detailing of similar incidents.

The Parable of the Good Samaritan

The children were asked to listen to a story that they had probably heard before and when it was completed they were asked some questions. They were not told the name of the story. When the story had been completed they were asked who they thought was the most important character in the story. One pupil replied 'the innkeeper', and asked why he chose the innkeeper his answer proceeded along these lines: 'Well, how would you like some beaten-up bloody person being dumped on you and you having to take him in. You wouldn't know if the other man would come back and pay you the extra money, so he had to have a lot of trust. That's why he's important.'

This statement led the pupils to discuss how they responded to people whom they saw to be hurt, but there was no reference to the Samaritan or the more traditional interpretations of the story. This caused me to reflect on the way teachers lead children to the conclusions they want and reject conclusions that do not fit their expected pattern. This type of response is a form of 'dissonance' – it jars upon the ear expecting a conventional learned answer. This pupil had started to explore his world through a parable without being aware how he was expected to respond. Do teachers lead pupils too rapidly to desired conclusions by suggesting, even in the title, those areas that are important? Should Bible stories, and all other activities, be allowed to develop towards a more open-ended conclusion? Is the process of learning and the act of engagement with the subject more important than the content, or at least the desired conclusion?

3

Some practical examples
from special schools

One of the features of teaching Religious Education is the necessity of establishing a point from which the subject can develop. This means the teacher has to create a learning structure for RE which is more like an inverted triangle. It will begin at the base point but the possibility for development will be readily available. One has to avoid thinking solely in content terms or modify one's approach from thinking of the quantity the teacher will *teach* to the opportunity for the pupils to learn.

Most of the following examples of work are taken from special schools, but not all are from ESN schools – some come from schools for the delicate and handicapped.

The schemes stretch across the age ranges. The terms 'early', 'middle' and 'upper' do not refer to the age range of the pupils but reflect their conceptual ability. Teachers reading through this work will be able to select and modify on the basis of their own schools, pupils, social environment and expertise. These samples though are based on classroom experience – they are actual lessons which should at the very least provide food for thought. Most of the teachers were not specialists in RE and the approach in this chapter will be to comment on each scheme from the point of view of the religious educator.

Firstly, however, there are three broad frameworks for the curriculum in the special schools. To some extent they are complementary though they have been devised separately in order to cater for schools and teachers who have a variety of different needs. They are, in effect, simple examples upon which each school could develop its own syllabus – one may go further and say they provide models for any school.

Frameworks for the curriculum

Throughout this book chronological labels for work schemes have been avoided. The stages 'early', 'middle', and 'upper' represent the *developmental level* of the pupil and each teacher will have to select what is most appropriate. These frameworks are neither comprehensive nor prescriptive, they are offered as an example of how the balance of work might be structured across the curriculum.

Early ability

1   Frequent use of *stories*; stories for pure enjoyment. Some may be from the Bible, some from other religious traditions, some would reflect the life style and interests of people who live in Britain as well as other countries of the world – all would be directed by the pupils' own understanding and what they draw from them.

2   There could be some *celebration* of festivals or major events and, while one would not expect every festival of every religion to be celebrated, the regular cycle of the year is important. Christmas and Easter (Christian), Passover (Jewish) and Diwali (Hindu) are possibilities and, of course, the regular celebration of family birthdays, holidays, meeting friends again after the holiday, etc. Much will depend upon each class but to celebrate is a feature of human life and pupils in this age range could be encouraged in this way.

3   Some introduction to, and use of, *drama* is appropriate. Most religions use drama through ritual, plays, the use of music and dance and so on. Some of the activities during the RE lesson could focus on the dramatic or the ritualistic aspects, for example how people use ritual when they meet each other. This can grow out of story and celebration with the opportunity for using stories from all cultures and music from Africa, for example.

Middle ability

1   During these years there could be again three different focuses. One could be *people*. What do they do? How do they dress? How do they pray? There are as many questions as there are people but the focus should be on human activity for people are interesting. One may take, in addition, some famous people, people who have helped, people

who have cared, and people from different cultures. There may be Biblical examples, historical or contemporary examples and perhaps also ordinary people who live in the neighbourhood of the school.

2   At this age the pupils could begin to look at *rules and rule-making*. It would be helpful if they could explore how and why rules come into being, whether they can be changed, who benefits from them. Virtually every religion has a set of rules, but they are not just concerned with morals, they are concerned with duty, obedience and faith, like food laws, attendance at Mass or the five Ks in Sikhism (Kes – uncut hair and beard, Kachh – short trousers, Kara – a bangle, Kirpan – a short sword, Kangha – a comb). In other words, the pupils should be helped to explore why some people (perhaps all of us in our own way) bind themselves to rules and why a person's religion often has special rules connected with belief and fellowship shared in community.

3   As mentioned earlier one may return to a theme and *festivals* would be a natural extension of the earlier theme of celebration. With younger children there was a concentration on celebration and perhaps some well-known festivals but now one could really explore what people do at festival time with stories of Mardi Gras in New Orleans, egg-rolling, egg-painting or other local festivals, local saints, etc. There are some excellent slides and videos available of festivals from various parts of the world. One extends the notion of celebration that surrounds oneself into the world of festival.

Upper ability

1   Teachers conscious that their pupils will soon be leaving school will need to support their self-identity and self-awareness. Topics that could be approached sensitively are *death, evil and pain*. Clearly the teacher must be prepared to discuss these issues with the pupil at any age, but in the context of RE there is the possibility of seeing how some people cope with these problems through faith, prayer and friendship. Some religions believe in an afterlife, others that one will be reborn on earth again, while others don't really concern themselves with life after death; however all try to explain and cope with the suffering apparent in life. This could provide a springboard for pupils to raise their own perplexity in relation to what they see,

2   As pupils grow older and acquire more confidence they could look more closely at *religion in their locality*. This could involve visits to places of worship, meeting and interviewing people, perhaps of a variety of religions and looking at different churches, mosques and so on in the area – what is the difference? At a time when they are getting ready to leave school an activity which takes them into the community has all sorts of benefits.

3   Related to the above, the school may already take part in some national fund-raising schemes and this could help the pupils to see how religions have a *social concern*. It depends on where the school is, but many Christian, Muslim, Jewish, Sikh, Hindu and Buddhist organisations have local offices. An interesting aspect is to note how Jews, Muslims and others are involved in voluntary work especially over Christian holidays.

More examples of how to devise an RE curriculum to run across school years and terms is provided through the following diagrams. These schemes offer a complementary approach to that suggested above. The developmental age of the pupils runs horizontally while the length of time spent on each theme runs vertically. It is a very helpful example of how themes may be set out to indicate the whole RE programme. These frameworks beg a number of questions. It is easy to fill in a grid with a list of words but what do they mean? What does the teacher understand by them? How will they be resourced and taught? All teaching, at any level and of any subject, requires a considerable amount of planning and research. One can begin with a simple 'brain-storming' of how to approach the subject of, for example, 'Trust'. Having done that the teacher can sort out an approach and a method to develop from the resources available within or near the school.

Autumn term

$\frac{1}{2}$ term/$\frac{1}{2}$ term

(approximately)

	3 weeks	3 weeks	3 weeks	3 weeks
Early	Myself	My family Harvest	Friends (4)	Christmas (5)
Middle	Journeys (2) Autumn Rules	Harvest Creation Growing (1)	People at work Trust (16) Listening	Christmas (5/20) New life
Upper	Holidays Rules Conscience	Harvest Christianity today	Service Honesty	Christmas (20) Celebrations
Leavers	Family and relationships Rules Law and order	Harvest An aspect of Islam, Hinduism, Judaism etc. People's life styles	Religious buildings Ways of worship in a couple of religions	Christmas (20) Celebrations

Note: the numbers in brackets refer to those themes which are expanded in more detail later in the chapter.

Spring term

½ term/½ term

(approximately)

	3 weeks	3 weeks	3 weeks	3 weeks
Early	Birthdays	Growing things	Senses Colours	Easter (8)
		Caring (6)	Bible stories	
Middle	Seasons	Weather	Stories from the life of Jesus	Easter (8)
	Homes	Neighbours	Bible stories	
			Forgiveness	
Upper	Courage (19)	Seasons	Stories from the life of Jesus	Passover and Easter
	New year			
	New start	Being sorry	Bible stories	
Leavers	Energy and power	Signs and symbols	Stories from the life of Jesus	Passover and Easter
	Communication		Bible stories	

Summer term

$\frac{1}{2}$ term/$\frac{1}{2}$ term

(approximately)

	3 weeks	3 weeks	3 weeks	3 weeks
Early	Water Sea Living creatures	Thank you	Sharing	Helping (10)
Middle	Sharing Belonging Relationships	Responsibility Fears	Giving and receiving	Special days
Upper	Famous people Religious teachers	People at leisure	Life cycle Space Being human People can choose People are different People have needs	Responsibility
Leavers	Creation Achievement Maturing	Journeys Authority figures	Moral codes Honesty	Service to the community

Autumn term

$\frac{1}{2}$ term/$\frac{1}{2}$ term

(approximately)

	3 weeks	3 weeks	3 weeks	3 weeks
Early	Growing (1) (a) Change (b) Sequence (c) Recurrence Building	Our body (3) (a) Hands and arms, feet and legs (b) Eyes, ears, nose, mouth and teeth (c) Inside and illness	Friendship (4) (a) My friend (b) The picnic (c) Cele-brations	Waiting for Christmas (a) Presents (b) Waiting (c) Christmas
Middle	Loving and caring (13)	Me or myself (14)	Me or myself (14)	Sharing Christmas (5/20)
Upper	Helping (24)	The Good Samaritan (22)	Barriers	The Christmas story (5, 20, 25)
Leavers	Friends (25)	Friends (25)	Friends (25)	Celebrating
Inter-faith	Yom Kippur Id-ul-Adha Janamashtami	Sukkot Rosh Hashanah Navaratri	Sukkot Durga Puja Guru Nanak's Day	Guru Gobind Singh Diwali

Spring term

$\frac{1}{2}$ term/$\frac{1}{2}$ term

(approximately)

	3 weeks	3 weeks	3 weeks	3 weeks
Early	Caring for our life together (6)	Being sorry (7) Reconciliation	Helping	Easter (8)
Middle	Journeys (2)	Pilgrimage (11)	Pilgrimage (11)	Easter (8)
Upper	Suffering	Suffering	Courage (19)	Easter (8) Elements
Leavers	Living and loving	Living and loving	Living and loving	Easter (8)
Inter-faith	Chinese New Year Purim Sarasvati Puja	Baisakhi	Holi Pesach (Passover)	Pesach (Passover)

Summer term

$\frac{1}{2}$ term/$\frac{1}{2}$ term

(approximately)

	3 weeks	3 weeks	3 weeks	3 weeks
Early	Special days (9)	Seeing and hearing	Food	Families
Middle	Trust and faith	Believing (17)	Courage (12)	Giving
Upper	People	Relationships (21)	Signs and symbols	Obedience
Leavers	Other religions	Reconciliation	Prayer	Neighbours
Inter-faith	Ramadan	Shavuot	Buddha Guru Arjan Dev Lailat ul Qadr Id–ul–Fitr	The Bab Obon

One crucially important feature is to let go of the notion of failure. Teachers, just the same as pupils, are conscious of their own failure: failure to meet the pupil's needs, failure to achieve 'results' (whatever those may be) and failure measured by the professional respect of their colleagues. Clearly some work is necessary if one is not simply going to churn out the same material year after year, but resources are available and there are an increasing number of resource centres. Perhaps most important of all is coming to terms with failure. Not everything we do in the classroom will succeed but then not everything does in life. As long as one can balance success against failure and enable the pupil to find an equilibrium in this relationship one is performing a valuable educational service. Hence looking at a draft curriculum should provide a frame for sewing the fabric of one's teaching experience – the colours will come from the pupil!

To take one or two examples:

1   In the first framework 'Christmas' appears four times. It can be extremely difficult to bring some variety into the Christmas extravagance, for pupils have expectations too. One way of developing the theme might be to emphasise different aspects of Christmas with each year. The story of Christmas contains within it many themes for example 'Journeys', 'Birthdays', 'Dreams', 'Refugee', 'Parenthood'. One could take one of these themes each year and with the central story in mind, come to it from a different angle – one could, of course, look at the origins of customs that surround Christmas too. So the same topic need not be approached in the same way and the broadening of the approach allows for a diversity of method and, perhaps, a more integrative curriculum.

2   Also in the first framework, there is a considerable emphasis in the spring term on stories from the Life of Jesus. I never fail to feel a mixture of despair and frustration with this topic because little is known of the life of Jesus – in fact nothing except what is contained in the Gospels and they tell us very little. A more productive approach, but one for which the teacher would require some confidence, is simply to tell a story – a parable or a miracle for example – and encourage the pupils to discuss it. Don't worry about the moral or what you consider to be the main point, just allow the pupils to enjoy the story or dismiss it. They don't have to accept it; it has no hidden authority and the power of the oral tradition should be strong enough for them to continue to reflect on it from time to time.

  The Parable of the Prodigal Son may not be about the prodigal son (what does prodigal mean anyway?) and the pupils may be far more interested in what riotous living is or what it would be like to live in a pig-sty. Indeed the elder son or the father may be more interesting characters juxtaposing forgiveness and resentment. If stories from the life of Jesus mean this sort of stimulation, then we remove from the teacher any sort of personal commitment to the Christian story. In addition it puts aside the false notion that somehow we know how Jesus would have behaved as a 6- or an 8-year-old.

3   Many teachers who are not specialists in Religious Education would flinch from spending time teaching about Purim or Baisakhi, for example. They feel they simply do not have the information available. To some extent this may be the case and, as with any other topic, the

teacher will need to gather together a certain amount of information. However, much of teaching is about method – the skills and attitudes one wishes to develop in the classroom – and it is surprising how the imaginative teacher can, with fairly limited information, create the atmosphere and feeling of a festival. Many festivals have a story attached to them, many festivals are celebrated in different ways so there is no only way, many festivals have acquired cultural accretions which can be brought into the classroom. Celebrating a festival though should be fundamentally about atmosphere and feelings, particularly with pupils who are classed as slow learners.

Themes and schemes of work

This section is a collection of pieces of work either taught by teachers or devised by them with a view to teaching it in their class. The developmental ages suggested only represent a general guide. As referred to earlier the teachers will themselves assess the developmental age of their class and take from the suggestions what they consider to be most appropriate. Some schemes, however, do indicate the class size and the type of school in which they were taught. All these lessons have been taught in class.

1   Three areas should be developed as related to a religious education:
    (a)   motor ability – to develop co-ordination
    (b)   the cognitive aspect – to elicit understanding
    (c)   the affective – to encourage the emotional

2   In every scheme there should be four regular aspects of each lesson:
    (a)   coming together – gathering together for a purpose
    (b)   greeting
    (c)   doing something
    (d)   celebration

1   Growing (early)

Begin with change, then sequence, plants and seeds and finally buildings.

Method

Sit in a wide circle.

Sing simple greeting song – 'How are you?', 'Where are you?' (tune to Tommy Thumb).

Talk about seats and where one is sitting (with the teacher in the middle of the circle). Crouch down and slowly stand up straight. The pupils might curl up and then they could grow – stretching to the very top. Three different children who knew how to 'freeze' would show the others then they would all freeze, some curled, some stretched but all would stop. They would then compare and contrast the different shapes but remember that all were still growing.

There would be a quiet time to think about leaves, traces or a baby.

The above would be repeated two or three times.

If the pupils learn this change the sequence then visit the park to bring back something – plants, leaves, etc. Sing a collecting song e.g. 'The Wombling Song' by Mike Batt (*Apussikidu*, A. and C. Black, 1975).

Make something like a tree – it might take three lessons. Discuss how the tree would be protected. Then a period of quiet – sing a quiet song and reflect upon a tree growing from a seed – it is an individual.

The pupils write out their names and hang them on the tree 'We built the tree – we made it.' Now they move to plants and seeds in the classroom. Also the idea that animals live in trees. What do we live in?

So the pupil is growing, making things for others, exchanging and giving. They can measure each other, remember their birthdays and growing older – this would lead to the place of thanking and notion of prayer. The 'growing' theme could relate to different parts of the body, using expressive movement. Some plants have no water – what happens to them? Seeds growing in varying ways have different characteristics. This opens up the possibilities for drama, being cold, thirsty, etc.

2   Journeys (middle)

This theme uses the same methods and approach as the previous scheme of 'growing'.

1   There could be a discussion about moving, getting lost, going to a different school, travelling by bus and train.

2   Develop a sense of direction and orientation (up, down, left, right). They could also make a train to pull across the classroom with toys or pupils in it.

3   What were their feelings on a bus – in sunlight, in rain, what would happen if the bus broke down? The enjoyment of going to new places. This would develop the idea of the destination being a place of value. Again there is ample opportunity for drama, even a relay race. What games or songs can one play or sing on the bus? Do we feel joy on arrival?

4   Each lesson could be a journey (in a boat, on a train, or an imaginary journey) perhaps taking presents. Taking things with us for the journey – things needed for the journey. Sense of happiness and pleasure on arrival – use different modes of transport, flying, sailing, walking, cycling, etc.

5   Stories of people on journeys are many and religions offer good examples.

In both these examples, one would make a list of further materials and ideas e.g. book about seeds or journeys, paint, clay, etc.

3   Our body (early)

Aim

To help the children develop an awareness and appreciation of themselves and their bodies, and an understanding of other people.

This theme has been used with infants in a Special School for children with moderate learning difficulties, aged between six and nine. The topic was pursued in a series of small units, some of which lent themselves to being explored more fully than others. The work included practical and creative activities, songs and stories including some from the Bible, recorded follow-up work and a great deal of discussion.

1   *The body in general – an introduction*

Name unusual and usual parts of the body.

Play – Simon says . . .
Sing – Heads, shoulders, knees and toes
We all clap hands together

Draw round a boy and a girl and make life size collage.

Look in full length mirror with each child individually – children then draw and colour self-portraits with as much detail as possible.

2   Feet and legs

What do we use them for?

running, walking, jumping, hopping, skipping, etc.
(practise these movements)

Make a collection of various types of footwear, discuss their uses and what they are made of.

football boots, shoes, sandals, ski-boots, plimsolls, wellingtons, slippers, etc.

Draw round children's feet – sort and order according to length. Make footprints. Children use a cut-out of their foot for measuring objects around the room.
TV programme 'Watch' – measuring and the need for a constant unit of measurement (*Teachers Notes*, BBC Publications, Spring 1984).
Story – The King's Bed.

Think about those less fortunate whose legs or feet do not work properly.
Story – *Janet at School* (spina bifida) by Paul White published by A. and C. Black.

TV programme 'Watch' – Mrs Elaine Dale, a victim of thalidomide born without arms, manages to look after a family successfully using feet to cook, change nappies, etc.

3   Hands and arms

Name palm, wrist, index finger, elbow, knuckles, etc.
Look at fingers, thumbs – count them.
Finger plays – Tommy Thumb
                        10 Little Squirrels, etc.

What do we use our hands for?

feeling, writing, eating, playing, holding, pulling, pushing, driving etc.
(mime guessing games)

Draw around hands, paint them and cut out hand shapes – make large wall pictures e.g. flowers, trees with falling leaves (leaves are hand-shaped) and hedgehog. Hand prints, finger painting. Policeman visited school to talk to the children – took children's finger prints.

Sing – 'If you're happy and you know it clap your hands'
Story – Jesus laying on hands to cure Jairus' daughter (Luke 8:40-56)
Books – *Sense of Touch* in the Read and Do Series published by Arnold Wheaton
Touching by Nigel Snell published by Hamish Hamilton

Talk about textures – rough, smooth, hard, soft, prickly, sharp, etc.

Game – feel objects blindfolded and guess what they are
feel small objects in closed material bags and pair them

4 *Eyes*

Look at own eyes in a mirror and draw and colour them. Name iris, pupil, eyelashes, eyebrow, etc. and talk about the eye being like a camera and how it works in a simple way.

What can we do with our eyes?

looking, seeing, reading, watching TV, etc.
appreciation of the beauty of the world about us, shape, colour, form

Take children on a 'looking up' and 'looking down' walk around town/country. Make a collection of things to take back to school for closer examination.

Talk about lenses in our eyes and that some people need help to see more clearly to read, watch TV or see.
Look at school eye test, glasses of children in the class, and talk about the optician.

Talk about the blind whose eyes do not work. Visit to school from a blind person with a guide dog to help the children realise how the blind cope with daily life. Feel Braille.

Film – 'The Training of Guide Dogs' (from The Guide Dogs for the Blind Association)

School collect tin towards the training of a new guide dog.

Story – *Sally Can't See* by Paul Petersen published by A. and C. Black
    Eyes and Looking by Doug Kincaid and Peter Coles published by Hamish Hamilton
    Jesus and the Blind Beggar – Bible Story (Mark 10:46-52)
    The Six Blind Men and the Elephant – Indian Folk Story

Activities with the magnifying glass and mirrors
Tricks our eyes play – optical illusions
Visual memory games – Kim's Game
                        Remember   2/3/4/5/6   objects   or
                        pictures

5 *Ears*

What are they for?

Sounds bingo game – Edward Arnold tapes for cassette recorder
Pupils recognise a variety of small objects in metal containers by their sound.

Talk about the deaf.
Deaf person to visit the school if possible (we have a deaf child in the school so we looked at his hearing aid and children realised his difficulty in communication). Lip reading, signing. Explain link between hearing and speech.

Story – *Claire and Emma* by Diana Peter published by A. and C. Black
    Ears and Hearing by Doug Kincaid and Peter Coles published by Hamish Hamilton

Whispering Game
Auditory memory games – remember a sequence of numbers,
                        letters, objects
                        go to the shop and buy . . . what
                        did you buy?

6 *Nose*

What do we need a nose for?
Discuss link between nose, throat and ears.

Smelling games

    perfume, curry, coffee, cola, vinegar, lemon, cloves, etc.

Make a block graph to show smells recognised most.

Talk about animals' sense of smell and realise that blind people often develop this sense more than sighted people.

7 *Mouth*

Discuss tongue, teeth, lips, gums, etc. What can we do with our mouth?

    taste, eat, drink, talk, laugh, etc.

Tasting games: blindfolded guess what it is from the taste. Divide a variety of foods into nice/nasty or sweet/sour sets.

lemon	sugar
grapefruit	apple
vinegar	honey

Talk about things never to taste – fungi and poisonous berries, etc.

Make bread, butter, cheese, chapattis, etc. in the classroom and eat them.

Talk about those without enough to eat, famine, war, poverty.

Story – Feeding of the 5,000 with loaves and fishes and the idea of sharing (Mark 6:37–44)

Talk about Blue Peter Project to help those without fresh water and children may become involved with a similar project to help others.

Talk about communication by talking and emotions shown by expressions of the mouth.
Story and video film about Joey Deacon (BBC Publications).
(Our children became involved in a sponsored Helping at

Home Project to raise some money for St. Lawrence's Hospital.)

What makes you feel?

anger, happiness, sadness, boredom, etc.

8   Teeth
What are they for?

eating, biting, chewing, talking

BBC TV programme 'Watch' on teeth and their care
Story – *The Toothless Knights* (*Teachers Notes*, Spring 1984)
Collect food labels and make charts of good/bad foods for teeth.
Collect children's toothpaste boxes and find the favourite brand.
The dentist
Story – *Tom Visits the Dentist* by Nigel Snell published by
          Hamish Hamilton
          Teeth in the Starters series published by Macdonald

9   Inside our body
Look at a skeleton.
Look at and feel bones from butchers.
Listen to and sing 'Those bones, Those bones'.
Talk about dinosaur bones found buried.
What happens if you break your bones?

X-ray, plaster cast and then they heal

10   When our body doesn't work properly
Discuss illness and accidents. People who look after us.

doctors, nurses, ambulance drivers
the hospital, the surgery

Look at Doctor's Set (Fisher-Price) and discuss the various objects and their use.

stethoscope, thermometer, syringe, etc.

ITV programme 'My World' – autumn term 1983
Story – *Topsy and Tim visit the Doctor*

The above themes represent an implicit approach to Religious Education though they do bring out aspects of the study of religion that are important. The discovery of the body, the whole and its parts, creates an entry into learning, how different parts of life make up the whole. Perhaps, as with all approaches to RE that emphasise the implicit, it is absolutely important that the teacher should be sensitive to the religious dimension. This is why it is so necessary for a school to plan its syllabus with care, the teacher then slots into a particular teaching block, implicit and explicit approaches work off each other creating a tension which can often be a most exciting part of learning.

The following diagram and themes from 'friendship' to 'Easter' (4–8) are from a teacher in a special school not a denominational one. *They represent a Christian centred approach which may not suit every teacher or every pupil.* However, each one is a valuable contribution in terms of method and approach and teachers will adapt the content as they feel appropriate.

For teachers who feel this is far too Christ-centred, far too Christian in its assumptions, I would encourage them to look at the more general approaches upon which the themes are developed, like developing a sense of worth and value, tolerance, acceptance, community etc. If one accepts these underlying themes as central, then clearly the chosen topic need not have built-in religious assumptions. These few pages illustrate as clearly as anywhere how difficult it can be to distinguish nurture in the broad sense of caring for the pupils within a school and guiding their emotional and physical development, and nurture in the more limited religious application of assuming a faith and ensuring that pupils grow up within that faith.

With an already fairly established class I would have the following sort of timetable for the first two terms.

Autumn term	Friendship	**Celebrations** **Presents** **Waiting** – waiting for Christmas **Christmas** – God gives the world a gift
Spring term	Caring for our life together Hurts Being sorry Reconciliation	Growth New Life – Easter

Autumn term

Linking in with the Christian year, I think I tend to develop one aspect of the celebration each year, thus for Christmas I have done themes on 'mums' (with a group where everyone had one) and 'presents', leading up to God giving us his son, and every year something on 'light', waiting for Jesus, who gives light to Christian lives. The light theme also links with the Jewish feast of Hanukah, the feast of lights, but it is not something I have actually done yet. There seems to be a difficulty involved with Christmas, as too easily children can strongly identify with the baby Jesus theme and stop there, not seeing him as a living adult person, so I usually have a session on birthdays pointing out that we all have birthday celebrations but we are not babies now.

RE starts with helping the children to an awareness of themselves as persons, loved and valued. This moves out to an awareness of community in terms of friendships and human relationships within the class and the school. All have a part to play in creating a community of friends. Only when a human community, a network of relationships of love and acceptance and tolerance is starting to grow within the class do we move to the spiritual dimension of a relationship with God.

Within each class there is a corner which is a symbol of the community of the class. This is where the class gathers (the maximum number I have had is eight children and two adults) to celebrate being together in a more concrete form. Initially the corner is arranged with a focus of something beautiful like flowers, a picture, a candle. Flowers and a candle further create the symbol of somewhere special.

To take the theme of friendship, this would be explored at many levels and in many ways in the class day. Drama, language work, PE helping and so on all give the child an idea of what it means to be a friend and to love a friend. Only when the class has grasped something at this human level are they ready to explore the religious dimension in a formal session.

Here are a few of the ideas you might explore in seven or eight weeks on the theme of friendship:

$$
\text{Friends}
\begin{cases}
\text{are kind to each other} \\
\text{share their things} \\
\text{talk to each other} \\
\text{give each other presents} \\
\text{listen to each other} \\
\text{look after each other}
\end{cases}
\text{We belong to a family of friends}
$$

These sessions have been done over a period of about five years with a group of 8 boys and girls aged 7 to 12 and a mixture of ESN(S) and (M) ability.

4 Friendship (early)

This reflects a general approach to the theme, obviously there is ample room for flexibility.

The human experience

I have a friend called Ruth.
Last night she gave me a present, I have it here.
(show a photograph album)
It's a photograph album.
(describe album, letting children hold it and feel it)
I thought we could put *our* photos in it.

(bring out some photos of the children and put them in the album with the children's help)
(relive the experiences shown)
Do you remember when . . .

Deepening the human experience

(show picture of children working together)
(describe it, pulling out elements of co-operation, working together, enjoyment, etc.)
It's fun to be with a friend.
We are glad to be with our friends.
We enjoy being together.

Religious dimension

When we come here with our friends to our special corner, our friend, Jesus is with us also.
Jesus is our friend.
He is glad to be here.
He enjoys being here with you.

Proclaiming the Good News

Pick up the Bible with care and read:
From reading the Bible Jesus says

> You are all my friends
> I enjoy being with you

> (repeat)

Giving the message to each

Go to each person in the group, get eye contact, take their hands and say:

> (Name) Julie,
>> You are my friend
>> I enjoy being with you

Response to the message

1   Some quiet music
2   All sing song 'Thank you Jesus for being my friend'

We belong to one family

This was a sort of summing up session to the 'friendship' theme. Earlier on in the week we had had a class picnic and I had painted a picture of everyone at the picnic, writing in their names underneath. This picture was used in the session as the symbol of our friendship together.

The human experience

Show magazine pictures of children on a picnic, enjoying sandwiches, cake etc. Talk about these and let children look at them. Show picture of group picnic and talk about it mentioning each person, stressing the enjoyment, the togetherness, doing things with each other, how we planned for it, prepared it together.

Deepening the human experience

Yes it's good to be with our friends
It's fun to enjoy ourselves together
Everyone helps to get the picnic together
Everyone helps to carry the food and rugs
We go out together, and everyone has a nice time together

Religious dimension

We are friends together in God's family
We *all* belong to God's family
We *all* have a place in God's family
We are happy to belong to God's family

Proclaiming the News

In the Bible we read about Jesus and his friends:

> One day Jesus went out with his friends. They took some bread to eat and some wine to drink and they had a picnic. Jesus and his friends really enjoyed themselves and Jesus said 'I am happy to be with you. I am happy to be with my friends.'

Giving the message to each

(Name) I am happy to be with you
      I am happy to be with my friends

Response

After the message has been given to each person in the group:

1   Quiet music
2   Sing song 'Jesus is my friend'

5   Waiting for Christmas (early)

Exploration of the waiting theme (before session)

Occasions when the children have to wait.
Waiting for dinner – getting ready – laying the table
                                    washing hands
                                    sitting down etc.

Waiting for the bus.
Waiting for a friend coming – welcome – we're happy to see them.
Waiting for a baby to come – we've got a large, young population
on the staff so this is well within the children's understanding.
Themes involved – patience, getting ready, pleasure.

The human experience

I was waiting for you all this morning.
I was looking forward to you coming into class.
(mention each by name)
I was looking forward to seeing . . .
You were waiting to come also.
(talk a bit about what the children wanted to say when they came in,
what they like doing)
I am waiting for Christmas.
I think . . . is waiting for Christmas too.
(mention each)
We are waiting quietly.
We are getting ready.

Deepening the human experience

When we think of Christmas coming we are pleased.
We are waiting.
We are all friends together.
Friends waiting for Christmas.

Religious dimension

Here together around our special corner.
We are waiting.
We wait quietly.
. . . waits quietly.
We get ready to welcome the birth of Jesus.

Proclaiming the News

In the Bible Jesus says:

> I will be coming soon
> I am coming to be your friend

Giving the message to each

(Name) Jo, I am coming
> I am coming to be your friend

Response to the message

Sing to the tune of 'Happy Birthday':

> We are waiting for you
> We are waiting for you
> We are waiting for Jesus
> We are waiting for you

Preparation in class – light and dark

Night and day, what it's like in the dark, being scared, not knowing what's there, not being able to find things. Creating experiences when the children are in the dark, being blindfold, playing games e.g. keys game, blind man's buff etc.
Dark pictures, light pictures, dark colours, light colours, lights, electric lights, candles, torches, etc.

The human experience

I have made a box which is devoid of light, at the back are stuck pictures of each of the children, at the front is a hole to look through but not enough light to be able to see the pictures. Inside is a light, when it is switched on the whole box is lit up and you can see. I let each child look into the box when it is dark and then switch on the light for each.

Deepening the human experience

When it was dark you could not see.
There was no light, you could not see.
You wanted to see the pictures, but you couldn't.
When I switched on the light you could see.
You could see your picture . . . (name each).
We need a light to be able to see.

Religious dimension

Christians are waiting for Christmas.
Christians are waiting for Jesus coming.
Christians are getting ready for Jesus coming.

Proclaiming the Good News

In the Bible Jesus says:

> I am the light of the world
> If you are my friend you will not be in the dark
> You will have my light

Giving the message to each

(Name) Julie, You are my friend
             I give you my light

Response

Sing 'Walk in the light' (adapted)

6   Caring for our life together (early)

Classroom activities

Caring for animals	Watering plants
Tidying up	Being kind to others
Washing tables	Caring for them

The human experience

Show children a picture of someone painting a door or clearing up.
Talk about the picture (we linked the painting picture with the
painters that we had had in school and how you need to take care of
woodwork).

Deepening the human experience

We care for our classroom.
We put things away.
We enjoy being in our class together.
We enjoy being with our friends.
We take care of our classroom.
We take care of our friends.
We come to our special corner to share that life together.
We come to be with . . . (name each one).
We come to listen to the Bible word.
We listen together.

Proclaiming the Good News

In the Bible Jesus says:

>Make your home in me as
>I make mine in you
>Grow in my love

Giving the message to each

(Name) Jo, I live in you
>Grow in my love

7 Being sorry – reconciliation (early)

Inevitably we aren't always friends! Sometimes it can be very difficult because you reach an impasse where children really dislike another child and show it and it seems that no amount of exhortation to be kind, 'how would you like it . . .' etc. does any good. I keep on talking to them about it when the occasion arises and keep saying the same things about being friends, being kind, we are all friends together and hope something sticks. The following is the bare outline of a reconciliation session to bring some of these things out in a more explicit way. Sometimes I think it is good to celebrate reconciliation in a more formal way. This session presupposes a lot of pre-classroom work when the occasion arises.

Human dimension

Show pictures of children (out of magazines) playing happily together. Then a picture of a child on his own crying. Point out he is sad, he has no friends, his friends have left him alone, it isn't nice not to have friends.

Or a child alone – someone has kicked him, he is sad, he is crying that wasn't very kind.

Or pictures of children kicking, biting, pulling hair etc. (home drawn cartoons) talk about them and the things we do sometimes that make others sad.

Deepening the human dimension

We are all friends here.
We don't kick or bite, or act nasty.
It makes others sad.
We say I'm sorry I have made you cry.
I am sorry you are hurt.
I won't do it again.

Proclaiming the Good News

In the Bible Jesus says:

> You are all my friends
> Be kind to each other

Giving the message to each

(Name) Shane, You are my friend
            Be kind to the others

Response

Shake hands with each person in the group.
I'm glad you are my friend
(encourage children to do the same)

Note: I find the Jean Vanier book *I meet Jesus* (Les Editiones Paulines, 1981) very useful for pictures. As well as having line drawings of biblical (New Testament) material, there are simple up to date drawings, some portraying handicapped people and their work, work centres, etc.

8 Easter (early)

I find the historical story of Easter too difficult for this age group to cope with, the concepts involved seem too hard; when you don't really understand death, to cope with someone coming alive again is very confusing. I have also had the experience of a child being obsessed (because of home teaching) with the physical gruesomeness of the story, so I tend to concentrate on just one aspect, that is 'new life'.

Classroom experience

Growing seeds
Baby animals, chicks etc.
Tadpoles
Bulbs
Buds, leaves, spring flowers

Human experience

Either
Show just growing mustard and cress.
Talk about them being filled with new life, bursting out of the seeds.

Or
Daffodils – showing them, feeling, smelling, touching, saying how beautiful they are.
Talking about how they grew from a bulb (show bulb and small growth).
Watering, growing. Each child has a daffodil to look at.
Put them in a vase with water in.
We put water in the vase to keep the flowers alive.
Now all the daffodils are together.
They look beautiful together.
At this time of year, Easter, we see lots of daffodils.
They make me feel alive.
I feel alive, full of life.

Deepening the human experience

We are together
I am happy to be with you . . . (name each one)
We are alive together

Religious dimension

When they see daffodils at Easter Christians feel full of life.
At Easter Christians thank God for new life.
Christians believe God gives *everyone* new life.

Proclaiming the Good News

In the Bible Jesus says:

> I have come that you may have life
> and have it to the full

Giving the message to each

(Name) John, I fill you with new life

Response

Sing 'Alleluia' (8 times)

Clearly it is difficult for a person who did not take part in these lessons or observe them, to criticise them. It does, however, appear that the pupils are being told things about Jesus that some parents would object to – there is an assumption of faith and the Christian faith in particular. Here the evangelical approach appears to have overcome the educational objectives, the pupils are required to learn verses which make definite statements of faith. However, one could easily take the basic principles involved and use them to a more educational end, e.g. belonging to a family, or various families, home, school, class, reading a story about friendship, exchanging greetings etc.

As with a number of the lesson plans in this book, readers may object to the confessional content but it is the principles, the lesson structure, that are of particular importance. The class teacher has tremendous importance in the selection and presentation of material. One of the major features of this type of approach is reinforcement and repetition so the pupil comes to recognise the structure of the lesson, feels secure and knowledgeable. For the pupil who has learning problems, the method or methods of learning have a greater importance than the content. The content appears to be the concern of teachers and parents, yet time and time again we recognise that learning stands a better chance of being productive if the methods are appropriate to the pupil and provide a variety of ways of learning.

9 Special days (early/middle)

(leading to an assembly)

What is a special day? Class discussion started with the teacher telling the class that the following Saturday was a special day for her as she was going to a wedding. All religions have special days, details can be found in the Shap Calendar of Religious Festivals – see address list at end.

Examples

James: The move back to Dad from the children's home.
Lydia: Dad's participation in the Remembrance Day Parade in London.
Nicola: Mum and Dad's Wedding Anniversary with a special dinner and wine.
Anders: His birthday.
Denis: Playing in the football team.

An assembly on special days

The children were asked to give their definition of a special day. One answer given was 'A day that was different to other days'. Other replies included holidays, birthdays, Easter, Christmas, etc. This opened the way for talking about our special days. Each child in the class read out what they had written about their special day.

This was followed by talking about other special days

Bank Holidays, birthdays, wedding days

I mentioned that the following Saturday was a special day for me, but, that it was much more a special day for the bride and bridegroom whose wedding day it was.

As this assembly was just before Christmas they concentrated on the special days of that period.

Mary's special day, when the angel appeared and told her she was going to have a baby.

Christmas day – the birth of Jesus.

Special day for the shepherds looking after their sheep in the fields. The angels appeared telling them the Christ child had been born.

Special days for the wise men
(a) when they first saw the new star in the East
(b) when they arrived in Bethlehem and saw Jesus

The children were then shown Christmas greetings in several languages and asked if they could read them, ending with a greeting in English which most of them could read and understand.

This approach to the festival of Christmas could be used for the birthdays of founders, messengers or leaders in other religions – Birth of Guru Nanak, Birth of Gautama, Birth of the Bab. The content will change but the concept of a 'special day' is familiar to most religious traditions and certainly to most pupils.

Close with the singing of a carol.

10   Helping (early/middle)

(leading to an assembly)

Aspects

(a)   helping people
(b)   being helped
(c)   helping others

Classroom discussions – each teacher with his or her own class (possibly following on from the action of a helpful child in the classroom) on the above aspects of helping.

The assembly

It was arranged that the younger children would dress up and act out:
1   Helping people – one class would write and say something, or read out a poem one by one as the younger children came on to the stage to show who they were, e.g. milkman complete with crate and bottles of milk.
    We chose the following helpful people:

postman	doctor	farmer
mum	nurse	teacher
dustman	police officer	school cleaner
bus conductor	milkman	

Song: When I needed a neighbour
    Were you there?
    (*Someone's Singing Lord* (A. and C. Black, 1973))

2   Being helped – teachers explained that the younger children were being helped to act out their parts by the older children doing their reading or speaking from the side of the stage.

3   Helping others – it was good for one class of older children to be helpful to the younger children in this way.

A prayer:
    Thank you for the people who help us
    Thank you for their kind hands
    Help us to be helpful to others
              Amen

11 Pilgrimage (middle)

Used with a class of twelve ESN(M) children, age range 10+ and 11+, predominantly 11+ (8 children), 7 boys 5 girls.

We did not normally have specific lessons for this project work – except for visits. Nor did we concentrate upon it every day.

Previous experiences

The older children had already been with the teacher for a year. During the summer term we had visited many places of interest in our immediate area – trackways, ridgeways, local ancient hilltop pond, two medieval churches, burial mounds, 14th and 15th century timber-framed houses, etc. Also visited the Weald and Downland Open Air Museum (Singleton, Sussex). Tried to get some idea of what it would have been like to live in such homes when they were built.

This particular class was very interested in TV 'History Around You' and appeared to have enjoyed this topic.

Aims

(a)   to attempt to make the children aware, in some respect, of life 'a long time ago' (we do not dwell too much on exact historical time)

(b)   to give the children some idea of the reasons for people making pilgrimages – especially to Canterbury

(c)   to give some insight into the understanding of integrity in standing for what is right – through the death of Thomas Becket – and of modern martyrs

(d)   to continue a year later – spring/summer terms – with environmental studies etc.

We used the BBC 'Merry-Go-Round' (Spring 1982) programmes as our starting point.

Trackways and ridgeways

The class enjoyed these programmes with the ghostly characters travelling along the old routes answering the questions of the presenter.

We went out and walked along the Ridgeway on nearby Farthing Down. We looked at the chalk showing through the grass – saw flints. Discussed what people probably used for building homes long ago and why. What they would have eaten. Why they lived on the hill-tops – where they obtained their water from, etc.
We walked over the humps showing the boundaries of the old fields.

Visit to Farthing Down again.
We looked at, stood on, had photographs taken by and drew some of the burial mounds.
We talked about the people buried there. Who were they, how did they die etc.? Discussed and imagined Saxon people who had had mugs, spears, shields, etc. buried with them.

Found *pictures* from old magazines etc. of some of the Saxon burial mounds and contents.
Tried to think of why they had their belongings buried with them. Do people do this now? What happens when people die? What do we think/hope happens to them (heaven)? Were those Saxon people Christians?

'Merry-Go-Round' BBC TV programme on 'Pilgrims' showed a pilgrim en route from Winchester to Canterbury. It covered hospitality, food, travel, companions, clothes and of course the reason – to visit the shrine of St. Thomas.

Chaldon Church

Very isolated old church with medieval wall painting showing the ladder of Salvation. Discussed building materials – flint, wood, some stone. Looked at the graves. What are churches for? Went inside – looked at the old worn step – what did that mean?

Looked at the wall painting – discussed why it was there (near Pilgrim's Way) – told children that it was to show people who lived hundreds of years ago how they should *not* behave (cheats and thieves and drunkards are all suffering horrible fates, angels and Jesus as a lamb up above in heaven). Talked about how people then could not read the Bible so pictures were painted or windows made to teach them.

Tried to imagine how people would have felt looking at it.

Do Christians now believe that God punishes us? Discuss. Also how do we know what God wants us to be like?

Looked at the church Bible – children read some verses with help. Talked about the church – font, altar, etc.

Very large picture begun in art lessons in class – hills, tracks, woods (tissue paper etc.). Chaldon Church and pilgrims drawn, coloured and cut out to be stuck on.

Had visited the library and borrowed many books on pilgrims, Thomas Becket, knights, monasteries, Life in the Middle Ages, castles, homes, farming, etc. The children frequently looked at these – asking many questions – what is happening in this picture etc.?

Very small, ancient town of Canterbury drawn and stuck on behind some woods. Windmill, farm, castle, manor, stocks, etc.

Pilgrims copied from various pictures and stuck on. The children's own drawings were fascinating and as their pilgrims were all sizes, we were able to form them into a procession with some sort of perspective.

Using various illustrations from library books, etc. we talked about Thomas Becket and the King – how they had been friends and why Henry made Thomas his Archbishop. I tried to explain how Thomas and the King had disagreed and how Thomas did what he thought was God's will. Talked about consciences. Discussed how we know when we are doing right or wrong, etc.

Pictures of the death of St. Thomas looked at. Talked about how the King felt afterwards and what he did to show his sorrow.

I went into more detail about death of Thomas – they were absolutely fascinated. They acted out the story.
We looked at *Ordnance Survey maps* of our area – noted the key.
We found the school, Farthing Downs and the tumuli, Chaldon Church and the Pilgrim's Way, etc.

Canterbury Cathedral

Using a road map we worked out a route to Canterbury. With string and a calculator we measured the distance and converted it into kilometres (we were just one kilometre in error).

The headmaster drove us in the mini-bus to Canterbury for a guided tour of the Cathedral. Our guide was exactly the right person for our party! The Cathedral Guided Tours Office had obviously given a good deal of thought to our needs and hopes. The Reverend Kemp showed us the Cathedral as a church, a great building and a place of pilgrimage. He explained the great teaching window – the poor man's Bible – showed us where St. Thomas' tomb had been, where the shrine had been built, etc. and why people came to visit it.
He showed the children the worn steps, and the miracle window and he explained some of the stories depicted in it.
The children were shown where St. Thomas had died – and were told what had led to his murder – why St. Thomas had not run away etc. Then we were shown the martyrdom and the children realised that people are killed even today for doing what they believe is God's work.

Follow-up work

We wrote letters to thank Mr Kemp for showing us around the Cathedral and he sent us a card back – much to the delight of the class.
Some children wrote about St. Thomas, his death, miracles, the Cathedral, etc. This work was mounted and put on the wall near our large collage.

Other work done during this project

We talked about what it would have been like to live in a village or town in medieval times – sickness, food, farming, poverty, etc. The children were fascinated by toilet arrangements especially the thought of a midden (dung heap)! Comparisons were made between the life of the rich and poor.

These discussions went on during the art lessons when deciding what to include on our picture!

We also talked about priests and how powerful the church was. Crime and punishment – we had stocks on our picture. Lightly touched on the feudal system – a manor house was also included. Worked out how timber-framed houses were built, finding bent trees, etc.

Castles and knights were studied by some boys. 'Ivanhoe' was on TV at this time. As our 'Merry-Go-Round' pilgrim had eggs for her protein, and as Lent was near we talked of Lent, repentance, forgiveness, etc. as part of what medieval people experienced. Made pancakes and ate them, also bread. Talked of Easter and eggs again (Easter pictures and stories were *not* excluded during this project).

An outline of the project is given on page 94:

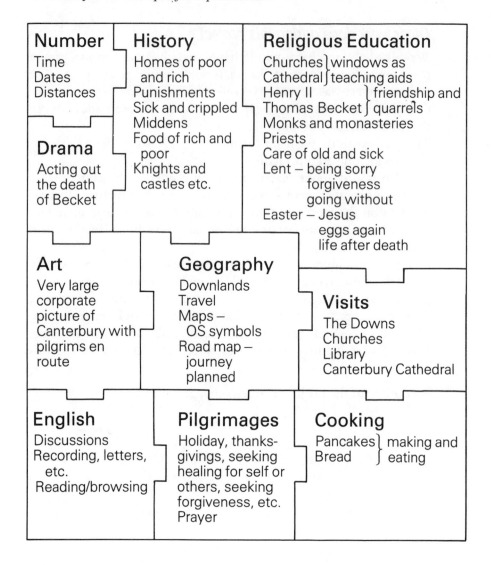

Number	History	Religious Education

Time
Dates
Distances
	Homes of poor
	  and rich
	Punishments
	Sick and crippled
	Middens
	Food of rich and
	  poor
	Knights and
	  castles etc.
		Churches ⎱ windows as
		Cathedral ⎰ teaching aids
		Henry II ⎱ friendship and
		Thomas Becket ⎰ quarrels
		Monks and monasteries
		Priests
		Care of old and sick
		Lent – being sorry
		      forgiveness
		      going without
		Easter – Jesus
		      eggs again
		      life after death

Drama

Acting out
the death
of Becket

Art

Very large
corporate
picture of
Canterbury with
pilgrims en
route

Geography

Downlands
Travel
Maps –
  OS symbols
Road map –
  journey
  planned

Visits

The Downs
Churches
Library
Canterbury Cathedral

English

Discussions
Recording, letters,
  etc.
Reading/browsing

Pilgrimages

Holiday, thanks-
givings, seeking
healing for self or
others, seeking
forgiveness, etc.
Prayer

Cooking

Pancakes ⎱ making and
Bread   ⎰ eating

Comments

1 The project went on rather too long, because the actual conclusion – the visit to Canterbury Cathedral – could not be arranged
   until fairly late in the summer term.

2 The less able children and some of the girls did not gain as much
   as the more able boys – who appeared to really enjoy it.

3 Visits were all very valuable. Children tend to 'open up' when out of the classroom. They all enjoyed meeting other adults and responded by asking questions – usually pertinent.

4 Books from the library were frequently dipped into. Library visits were enjoyed and the children's librarian made us very welcome. Several children joined their local libraries as a result.

5 We had a Sri Lankan student from a local hospital with us for most of this time and he told us about pilgrimages made in his country. We also touched on pilgrimages to the Holy Land and to other shrines in this country.

6 The reasons for the quarrel between Henry II and Thomas Becket were rather too difficult for many of the children to comprehend, but I think that the fact that Thomas was willing to die because he believed he was doing God's will was understood.

This is an excellent example of an integrated topic which, while taught to special school pupils, can easily be adapted for the primary school. The teacher in question has thought about the aims of the topic and the variety of learning methods that could be employed. Even so she does acknowledge that the less able gained least from the exercise perhaps they did not feel they had particular objectives in front of them. This imaginative topic indicates how difficult it is to balance the requirements of the individual pupil, even in a small class. One can understand how the inter-related activities may have become too much for the least able pupils, who might have felt more secure with fairly limited tasks, repetitive even, which would have made their own progress measurable to them.

This appears again and again – one of the marks of progress with the pupil with learning difficulties, of any age in any school, is the actuality of recognising their own achievement. The pupil *must* succeed. He or she is only too familiar with the notion of failure, or even worse of non-comprehension, so in planning any activity with the less able one has to give clear, precise instructions and ensure that the stages of progress are understandable and achievable.

The question of assessment in the strict sense doesn't arise in this topic though the teacher was aware that there were two particular problems: the topic went on for too long and some pupils didn't get much out of it. The first problem is one with which all teachers are familiar, even for experienced teachers it is desperately difficult to ensure that the timing is right, experience helps but it is not always enough. The second problem is much more difficult to define because it is not certain how effectively one can ever assess visits, for example, in the long term. We may feel pupils did not take from the visit that which we felt they should, but they may take other things – a sense of colour, of space, which will not emerge for some time. Again, it does depend on the teacher being clear about aims and objectives and recognising that some objectives will not be assessable in the conventional sense.

12   Courage (middle)

Rescue services around the coast of Britain.

Coastguard – provides vital link between ship and shore, monitors a section of coastline and is able to alert appropriate services quickly

Lighthouses and lightships – warn shipping of dangerous rocks or sandbanks; however, men are slowly being replaced by automatic lights

Royal Naval Rescue Service – brave men who rescue people in all weathers from sea and cliffs, helicopters have a crew of four – two pilots, winch, winch operator – brief description of each job, mention maintenance engineers on the ground who help to keep helicopters in first class condition, emphasise teamwork

RNLI – perhaps the bravest of all, mention Penlee lifeboat disaster before Christmas 1982, ask if anyone knows what RNLI stands for

(All the above should be illustrated and children can read a short paragraph about each one.)

Introduce a play about a famous lifeboatman – Henry Blogg – who came from Cromer. Henry was a coxswain of the Cromer lifeboat in 1917 and was involved in many rescues. One particular night he rescued two separate crews. Emphasise that most of Cromer's young men were away fighting the First World War and many of the crew were over seventy years old. They had to launch the lifeboat twice on a dreadful night – their lifeboat was not modern but a rowing boat with sails – and managed to rescue all the sailors.

During his lifetime he and his crew saved 873 lives (illustrate with chain of 873 matchstick men).

13 Loving and caring (middle)

Aims

(a) to explore how loving and caring play a part in the world in which we live
(b) to help the pupils to understand the importance of such concepts in religion

Method

1 Tell stories and act them out so that the pupils learn the story and enjoy the drama (allowing a fairly liberal interpretation) e.g.

Naaman the Syrian	(2 Kings Ch 5)
Ruth	(Ruth Ch 1-4)
Joseph	(especially Genesis 44-50)
Jesus	(John 11:17-44)
Zaccheus	(Luke 19:1-10)
Philemon	(Epistle of Paul to Philemon)

Discuss how these examples are of different people caring for each other and for the world they lived in regardless of each other's religion, race, occupation or status. There are many stories about people in every religion – help in resourcing these can be found in the address list and by writing to the Shap Working Party.

2 Then move to an awareness of how each person is part of a caring family whether we have parents or not or however old we are. List ways of showing love and care particularly in a family situation, e.g. food, clothes, discipline, toys, talking with us, playing with us.

3 Continue this only transpose it to love and care in school, e.g. helping, consideration, rules, sharing.

4 Then move to the more difficult question of caring for those whom we don't like as well as those we do, e.g. elderly grandparents, someone who has to share your bedroom.

5 How do we show concern for people we have never met – by collecting money, giving something, etc.

Resources

Read *Melissa* by Diane Baumgartner (Triangle/SPCK, 1982) and/or others in the series, in simplified form to the class. It is the story of a severely handicapped baby adopted into a family.

People whose jobs have a caring aspect, e.g. doctors and nurses, firefighters, school cook, etc.

Caring for animals, our pets and the environment (wild birds in winter).

This theme would involve various classroom activities, e.g. scrap book, drama, based upon caring for specific groups of people and animals as well as exploring loving and caring through discussion and story. The theme could then be developed into an assembly.

Pets we have and care for *(a development out of general theme)*

Story of lost sheep told by teacher – then show how a shepherd's crook is used. Ask the pupils 'How do we show love and care for our pets?' Varied answers come back – 'We feed them, wash them, comb them, play with them, take them for walks and simply love them.' Each class could then list all the pets kept by number and variety.

14 Me or myself (middle)

(roughly one term's work)

This was with a class of thirteen. There were five 'church-going' children, so it was decided to use this fact in the project, which was to be RE based, though of course it incorporated other subjects – English, some number work, art, drama, TV, etc.

Objectives

1 To encourage the children to be aware that, although they share many characteristics and features:

    (a) their experiences produce feelings within themselves that are shared by others, that these feelings are common and acceptable, especially the negative ones: fear, anger, etc. By discussion to try to understand results of these bad feelings (behaviour problems, etc.)

(b) each one is still very much an individual

(c) they have various allegiances – to family, friends, class school and groups – and that five of our class have a church allegiance.

2   To visit and look around the churches attended by the five church-going children and to meet the priests or pastors

3   To ascertain the reason(s) why these children and presumably their parents attend church/Sunday School

4   To discover what people do in the church

5   To lead on to the Christmas story/festivities

Using the *Tinder Box Assembly Book* (A. and C. Black, 1982) (page 4), we begin by considering 'what it feels like to be me'!

When asked 'Who knows you better than anyone else?' it took quite a while for the answer 'me' to come.

I read them some poems:

'My Puppy'	from *The Young*
'Jemima Jane'	*Puffin Book of*
'Upside Down'	*Verse*
etc.	edited by Eleanor Graham

We discussed likes, dislikes, things which make us happy or annoyed.

'Feelings' seemed to be included in almost every TV schools programme we saw. 'Ways with Words' (ITV), 'The History Trail' (BBC), 'Zig Zag' (BBC), even 'Look and Read' (BBC) incorporated or explored experiences and feelings, e.g. being wrongly blamed, moving to a new house, starting at a different school, etc.

The class were very easily able to enter into the feelings of others.

We ran a sponsored 'Make an effort to help others' to raise money for the Joey Deacon Memorial Fund and help set up a communications unit at St. Lawrence's Hospital, Caterham, which is local. We borrowed the video film 'Joey' (BBC Publications) from Joey's friends and interpreters Ernie and Tom. All the school saw the film (in two sessions) and much discussion and questioning followed. Dr. Geoffrey Harris brought Ernie and Tom to an assembly to collect the money raised. The children were able to meet and talk to Ernie (in wheelchair) and Tom.

Filmstrip 'Me' (Philip Green Educational Ltd.) stressed that:

(a)   no-one is exactly like anyone else, though there are many similarities
(b)   differences – size, colour of skin, hair, etc.
(c)   our feelings – positive and negative
(d)   taking care of ourselves – how? ⎫ ties in with 'Good Health'
(e)   taking care of others – how?   ⎭ ITV

Pictures of children's faces depicting various feelings were shown in this filmstrip so we tried acting out feelings – good and bad. The class entered into this with great gusto. It was interesting that the little sketches depicting the negative-type feelings like fear were made to end in a positive way, e.g. a lonely person befriended, etc.

Work was going on concurrently making individual scrap-books entitled 'Myself' or 'Me'. In these the children drew their families, naming all the members, the class, the school, etc. We talked about St. Nicolas then coloured a picture of the school badge and stuck that in.

Photographs of the class and of each child were taken. These were mounted in the classroom on a wall. Under each photo was stuck a piece of writing about themselves, to include name, age, date of birth, family, etc. and any group allegiance – including the usual football teams, chess club, choir, recorders, any uniform organisation and in the case of five children a church. (These will eventually be stuck in the front of their scrap-books.)

We spent one lesson, using mirrors, with the children comparing themselves with their classmates, noting verbally the similarities and differences in physical appearance. They watched each other's eyes in sunlight then in shadow, noting similar reactions to changes of light. I recited the poem 'Noses' by Aileen Fisher (*Young Puffin Book of Verse*), already familiar to them. We tried to ascertain the relative positions of the facial features and then to draw/paint a friend, getting the various features in the correct places (still impossible for some).

We asked the local policeman, familiar in our school, to come and take fingerprints which could be stuck in the scrapbooks. This was an informal session with much chatting, but with our lenses the children could plainly see that their fingerprints were unlike those of their friends. The constable explained that this was the reason the police used fingerprinting, and went on to tell the children the various other means of identifying criminals that are used – blood, sweat, hair, etc. common to all but unique to each person.

Following up the policeman's visit we did counting of hands, fingers, etc. Made pairs of handprints and put them on the wall as counting aids – 2s, 5s, 10s. Discussed how useful hands were. Went on to more explicit RE. I asked how many hairs they had on their heads – could we count them etc. and went on to tell them that in the Gospels Jesus had said that God knows how many hairs are on their heads, that Christians believe that God cares for and about every single person and has made every one different, etc. One boy, Craig, said he did not believe in God. Rachael answered that it was true that God did exist 'In the Bible God made Adam and Eve out of one of Adam's bones' (Rachael goes to a Pentecostal church). Much discussion followed about (a) whether we all believe in God and (b) if Rachael believes what she says is true, must Craig also believe it etc.?

By this time we had ascertained which members of the class attended church, so we decided that it would be interesting to visit the various churches on Friday mornings or afternoons.

1   Joanne's church is in the middle of an older type of council estate. It is a daughter church of the local Parish church and is in the care of a Church army captain, who is young and full of life. He and his wife and Joanne's mother showed us around the church. We asked why people came to church and it was explained that because they believed Jesus died for all people they came to church to worship and pray and to thank God for Jesus. The church was compared to a home – there is a table where people eat and drink. The captain showed us the chalice and the wafers. He let the children eat a piece of a wafer if they wanted to – not all did! He told them that Joanne was to be confirmed and he asked her to explain why bread and wine were used – which she did, simply. He showed the class the organ and he played it so that they could sing. The children were given

squash and biscuits. We looked at the Bible, the font and had baptism briefly explained. The church bell was rung and we were asked why and when it was used, etc.   (about 1 hour).

2   Paul's church is bigger and on a newer council estate. The vicar asked each child's name and greeted them by name, saying how pleased he was that we had come. He had the children running around the church looking for pictures on kneelers. This was great fun and made them feel very much at ease. He then showed them around the church, the font, the banner, explaining and questioning. He used the Easter candle with its symbols and five studs to explain what Christians believe had happened to Jesus, the symbol of the cross, the studs representing the wounds. The two sleeping Roman guards remind people of the tomb in which Jesus was raised from the dead. The vicar explained how Christian people come to God's house each week to remember Jesus, how they believe that Jesus lives now, and that he is always with us. He told us that when he had come to know Jesus as a friend and helper he had become a much happier person. He talked about the importance of friends – our friends, Jesus's friends and Judas.

He went on to explain about the Last Supper with the bread and the wine, and how after the crucifixion the disciples understood what he had meant about the body and blood.

He also explained about the altar, the cloth and chalice, and how the people come up and kneel at the rail. He asked the children if they would like to kneel there – which they did – and said a prayer for them and a blessing which I felt was meaningful to them. He asked us to come back after Christmas to find out more about Jesus and all the children said they would like to.

(about ¾ hour)

3   Heloise is a Roman Catholic and attends a church quite near to the school. A young, very friendly priest showed us around. He told us how St. John the Baptist, after whom the church is named, was a strange man who had lived in the desert. Through questions and answers he encouraged the children to describe a desert, leading on to water, its uses, then he asked where water could be found in a church and why. He asked Heloise who in her family had been recently baptised and encouraged her to tell

her classmates about baptism. He showed them the altar and told them it was a table with a cloth for a meal. They knew by this time what the 'meal' consisted of. He explained that the people came on Sundays and acted out Jesus's last meal – the priest acting Jesus's part and the people his friends. He then showed the children the statues of Mary, Joseph, Jesus and the Crucifix and explained that these were to help people to remember. We then went round the carved stations of the cross, so the Easter story was again explained, this time pictorially.

We then sat on the carpeted altar steps and sang carols learned in school and action songs taught by the priest and a young woman with a guitar. We finished by singing the Lord's Prayer and by each child and adult lighting a candle. As the candles were handed to them the priest named each individual, and asked them as each one was lit who they wanted to be remembered before God. Again all joined in and seemed to enjoy the experience. After biscuits and squash we returned to school.

(about ¾ hour)

4   Rachael's church is a Pentecostal church in a rather dilapidated area of Croydon. Its congregations are so large that they have met for some time past in a larger Anglican church some three or four miles away on Sunday evenings. We visited the older building for obvious reasons.

The young pastor made us very welcome, but he did not know Rachael – perhaps due to the large congregations. He explained that their church did not need pictures in windows or on the walls, nor did they need a cross because Jesus was not on the cross, 'He is alive'. The pastor and two young women from a Bible College showed us around the building, the creche and the Sunday School room upstairs. The two girls sang us a song about giving your heart and living for Jesus. The pastor explained that he believed Jesus is our saviour and died for us to save us from our sins. The children asked questions comparing it with other churches, for example 'Do you use candles?' and he explained why not – the word of God in the Bible is all they need. Asked whether they used bread and wine to remember Jesus, he showed them the little individual glasses, but said they used Ribena instead of wine. He explained how they baptised people in a large sort of paddling pool as they did not have a proper baptism pool in the floor, but he did stress that babies and young children were not baptised, only adults or teenagers as in the New Testament. He gave each child a little book *Jesus My Saviour*, which emphasised sin and the fact that we deserve punishment unless we believe that Jesus died for us.

(about ¾ hour)

5   Christine attends a Seventh Day Adventist church with which I was unable to make contact.

The Church army captain and the two priests were very much in tune with our children, especially the two priests who knew how to draw information from the children. The class experienced being welcomed into churches, having fun, being told simply what Christians believe by confessing Christians. They had the sacraments of Holy Communion and Baptism explained in each church and were told the Easter story in three different ways. They also experienced prayer in the churches. In two of the churches, they were treated very much as individuals, the priests calling each child by name.

After each visit the children wrote thank you letters. Paul's vicar wrote an individual reply to every child. This was wonderful for the children and after taking them home to show their parents they brought them back and stuck them in their books.

Christmas preparations/story followed.

'Me' or 'myself' is a big subject – it does represent a term's work. There are a lot of good ideas in this but one of the most interesting features is the way in which the different churches responded to the visit. It would have been useful to have listened to the pupils' discussions about each visit. There is much work with language that could and should arise from such a visit – it would follow as a natural corollary from the earlier discussion about belief in God.

One anxiety which teachers of all pupils demonstrate quite frequently is the way in which they do not allow the pupils to express their own ideas. Listen to pupils talking to each other and one can be amazed at the profundity of the discussion. Rachael and Craig talking together may have travelled a great deal further along the theological road than they would by hearing a parable and drawing a picture. We should take great care not to undervalue peer group work and be able to relax encouraging pupils to discuss with each other. Rachael and Craig's discussion of the nature of truth strikes me as being far more important than walking around a few churches. It would be more important to listen to their dialogue after the church visits to see if they had taken their thinking any further.

It can be a fault to assume that pupils' opinions are not really important because they do not fit in with, or relate to, adults' opinions. Elsewhere in this book we have referred to this as dissonance because the opinion of the pupil does not harmonise with the view of the teacher. Perhaps it is only with the truly dissonant pupil that learning really takes place. We will return to this point later.

15 Trust/faith and background to the New Testament (middle)

(Class of 5 boys and 4 girls – outgoing, lively children)

Following on from the Christmas story:

Aims

(a) to enable the children to experience trust, in however small a way, or to recall trusting from their own experience
(b) to gain or reinforce some background knowledge of the life of a boy or girl in Israel at the time of Jesus

Apparatus

Artefacts used by Jews in the practice of their religion.
Many large coloured pictures including synagogue, homes, people etc.
Books on background to the topic, e.g. NCEC 'Getting to know about' series – *Homes & Houses, Learning* and *Playing in Bible Lands.*
Boxes etc. for junk modelling.
A *Good News Bible* (Collins) is always available for reference, so that the children will realise where stories about Jesus are to be found.

Method

1   Using the 'Jesus of Nazareth' slides (set 1) (Bible Society), told story of Jesus's Passover journey to Jerusalem (Luke 2:41-52), discussed being lost, parents' feelings, children's own experiences, etc.

> Special journeys – reasons, feelings.
> Why Jesus went to Jerusalem – temple briefly mentioned – noted reputed size etc. from slides.
> Synagogues – general features – segregation of sexes in some synagogues.
> Children tried on a Jewish prayer shawl and cap, looked at a child's picture/story book written in Hebrew.
> School, etc. discussed briefly.

2   In topic fashion tried to gain some ideas of what a village might have been like in Israel during first century CE (AD).

> Compared general look of homes and villages then with those of the children in the class – shapes of houses/roofs, outside stairs, windows, water, light, power.
> Noted water/oil jars, bed rolls, animals, etc. Parable of the Lost Coin told/read from St. Luke (15:8-10) and acted – children enjoyed this.

3   From pictures discussed jobs people did – women's work, water carrying, wells, etc. Mentioned man who fetched water (Mark 14). Also talked about games and toys with which children played – compared them with present day pursuits.

In order to be able to make junk models, again looked at pictures of houses, noted furniture, etc. and hand mills for grinding corn (we had previously visited working windmill and a farm where there is a handmill and corn to grind). Talked about sleeping arrangements/beds.

Introduced story of paralysed man (Luke 5:17-20) – tried to imagine what it would be like to be paralysed.

Tried to encourage class to act out story – but they would not (unusual for this group). We played 'trust' game – see *Using the Bible in Drama* (Bible Society) – in which one person stands with others round central person, keeping eyes closed and feet on one spot, is passed round or back and forth between rest of group.

All realised that they had to 'trust' their peers. The group were very supportive and trusting of each other except one child who would not join in at all. ('Trust' games can be disturbing to some children and should be used with care – teachers should have experienced them themselves and should be sensitive to the class they teach.)

Talked about who we trust and why – mothers, fathers, doctors, nurses, etc.

4 Recalled story of paralysed man – discussed how he must have felt about his friends – trust. Children were encouraged to shut their eyes, pretend they were like that man and decide who they would ask to take them to Jesus. All chose their mothers, some fathers, some family members, some friends – reasons why they had chosen the people they had.

> Occasions remembered when they had had to trust people. The importance of good friends – what a good friend is/should be.
> What the paralysed man's friends did when they found they could not get into the house to Jesus – their trust/faith that Jesus would help their friend.

Suggested acting the story – this time they did and enjoyed it!

5 Children realised that all who came to Jesus for help must have trusted him and reasons why this might have been were discussed.

Models of houses made in art sessions – holes made in roofs of some!

No written work was done on this particular theme.

16 Believing (middle)

(based on 'St. George and the Dragon' by Dinah Starkey in *Monsters, Dragons and Sea Serpents* published by Kaye and Ward, 1979)

1 Tall Story Game.

Children try to outdo each other, e.g. *my* car, *my* best present, etc. Claims tend to become rather outrageous but this only adds to the game.

Discussion – when do we need to be believed?

Improvisation of some ideas suggested in discussion:
    making an emergency phone call
    explaining why goods don't work
    telling teacher or mum why you are late

Children work in pairs or small groups. They only demonstrate their work if *they* wish to – the emphasis is on experience rather than display.

Evaluation with children – did all the children manage to convince their partners? If not, why weren't they believed?

2   Read part of 'St. George and the Dragon'.

Discussion – why do children think the people wouldn't believe the shepherd boy? What kind of people lived in the town?

Development – teacher to assume a role, e.g. shepherd or mayor – children are allowed to choose a role for themselves and to join in a market scene:
    the farmer has brought cows to sell
    his wife is selling cheese
    young girls are buying lace and ribbon

Any child who finds it difficult to select a character can be helped to assume a role by teacher in role, e.g. 'Hello Mrs Brown, I haven't seen you for a while. Can I help you set up your stall?'

When the town is established teacher can then introduce the idea of the dragon. Do the people of the town believe in it?

Volunteers are asked for to look for the dragon. Will they send someone alone or all go together?
How do the people feel when the king refuses to send help?
Mayor to call a meeting of whole town to discuss feeding the dragon.

Conclusion – read or act out end of story.

3   Classroom discussion: how often do we accept as true things that we can't see?

We can't see electricity but we expect the lights to work when we press the switch.
We can't see other planets but we know they are there.
We can't see friendship or courage but we can recognise them in others.

4   When preparing for our class assembly the class decided that they wanted to talk about St. George. I asked what had impressed them most and they said his courage and the fact that he refused to take a reward.

The children thought he was a soldier and we talked about bravery.

We talked about the Crusaders who left everything to defend the land of Jesus's birth.

We linked the flag of St. George with the emblem of the Crusaders.

This gave the children a basis for *their* assembly. (We could have chosen other topics e.g. belief, trust, courage, etc. which were explored in the drama sessions.)

5   *Assembly*

Focal point – a large St. George's flag painted by the class.

(The children acted out the story of St. George and the Dragon. We didn't have time to make a dragon costume so pictures of dragons were traced onto OHP transparencies and projected onto a screen which became the dragon's lair.)

Today we would like to tell you the story of a very famous soldier.
(Enter children dressed as Crusaders.)

I am a Crusader. I have left my home in England to fight in the Holy Land.

We heard about the brave deeds of St. George and want to be like him.

We wear his emblem and carry his flag.

Hymn: 'When a knight won his spurs'.

We still remember St. George today. He is our patron saint and we still use his flag.

17   Journey of life (middle)

(leading to an assembly)

The journey of life – this idea for assembly has been included not as a theme for RE but as an example of the way in which pupils can explore an idea through *drama*.

My aim was to allow the children to express their own ideas about right and wrong.

Preparation lesson

Introduction – we played a number of warm-up games e.g. Cat and Mouse – cat outside the circle must try to catch the mouse in the centre. All the children in the circle join hands and try to prevent mouse being caught.

Children were then divided into twos and labelled A and B. A was sent to get a chair and told to sit on it. B then had 2 minutes in which to get themselves on the chair. After 2 minutes A had to persuade B to relinquish his or her seat.

Discussion – children were asked to report back on their efforts to gain a seat. Who gave up easily? Who used threats or violence? Did anyone refuse to move at all? Why? Is it easy to say no?

Again split the class into small groups of 3 or 4. Take one child from each group to one side and explain that they must refuse to do whatever the others want to do. Tell the other children that they must persuade their friend to go on an outing with them. They must all go or all stay at home.

Give each group 3 minutes and see how many children have given in. Select another child from each group and reverse the instructions. This one child must persuade the others to play a particular game.

Discussion – was it easier to persuade one person or three people? Have the children ever been in trouble because someone else persuaded them to do something?

Improvise a couple of incidents related by the children.

Discussion – how could we prepare an assembly to show that it isn't easy to do what is right? Various ideas were suggested:

gangs
bullies
goodies and baddies

This idea caught the class's imagination and we talked about stereotyped good and bad guys. Someone suggested cartoon type devils with horns, tails and pitchforks.

We then talked about the kind of things we are often tempted to do, not commit big crimes like murder or bank robbery but the little temptations we face every day.

Each child was asked to contribute an idea as if they were persuading someone else e.g. 'Your mother will never know that you spent her change on sweets. If she asks say you dropped it.'

Development

One child was nominated to be the 'goody'. All the others elected to be 'baddies'. (They were so keen they gave up lunchtimes to make costumes.)

The goody walked across the hall, one by one the little devils tried to tempt him or her. 'Why not steal some sweets from the shop – no-one will see you.'

As each devil was rejected he or she ganged up behind the goody. After each temptation calls of 'Go on, why not? No-one will know!' get louder and louder. It became harder and harder for the goody to go forward.

Assembly

The children acted out the above improvisation.

Hymn: The journey of life

Prayer (written by child):

> Dear God, show us the right road to walk along and help us to say no when people want us to do wrong things. Amen.

18   Courage (middle/upper)

(an assembly for the whole school)

Aims

(a)   to explore the concept of courage on a personal level
(b)   to examine particular examples of courageous people in society

Method

1   Personal courage – discuss with the pupils situations where they need to demonstrate courage in school, e.g. standing up for oneself against a crowd. One would want to stress that acts of courage can be quite small. This would be reinforced by role-play using everyday situations where some courage is required.

2   One could then look at people in the news who have shown courage. A class scrapbook could be started with newspaper or magazine cuttings. Television frequently provides examples of people who have shown courage too.

3   People who have become famous because of their courage in times of difficulty e.g. Ann Frank, Father Kolbe, Douglas Bader, St. Paul, Gandhi, Martin Luther King, Mother Teresa, etc. This would mean telling the stories to the pupils, perhaps using some role-play, then moving on to a discussion about how *their* courage related to our own small acts of courage.

19   Sharing: an account of a Christmas assembly (middle/upper)

Christmas is usually a happy time. Why is this? Well basically, to be honest, it's a time when we receive presents and gifts.

We share things with one another.

But we don't just share things at Christmas time. We share things every day. Let's look at some of the ways we share.

We will look at how we share in school first.

Slides

Commentary – we share together in the classroom. We help each other with our work, indeed sometimes we might find this work impossible without helping each other.

We also share together when we play games. We share our skills, different talents and our company.

At home we share meals together. Good food, drink and good company. Mind you we can share in other things. Even the head teacher helps wash the dishes!

Show slides of head teacher washing the dishes.

When we give a little thought to it, it is obvious that we not only like to share but in order to survive we need to share.

Think how many people need to share together. In order to build a house, for example, we need architects, bricklayers, plumbers, electricians, gas fitters, carpenters and so on. The list is almost endless. Can you imagine how big London would be today if people had *not* learned how to work and share together? Why, there might not even be a London at all.

In order to get the most out of life we have to share together, indeed in order to get the most out of everything. We can only expect to get out what we put in.

Here is a little sketch acted out on stage to illustrate this point:

The Story of the Four Beggars (acted out on stage)

One afternoon four beggars met together behind an old burnt-out building. They had been begging and scrounging around all morning. One had managed to scrounge a piece of meat, another a bit of cabbage, another a few carrots and the last one a very large potato. They fell to talking about how each of them was going to enjoy his own little snack, but they all agreed that by themselves they were pretty miserable. They all thought as one, 'Why not share our little bits of food together and make a nice warm soup?' So they all agreed to meet that evening in an old hut that they often used to sleep in.

It was dark when they arrived at the hut but the glow of the cooking fire enabled them just to see the pot. They each decided to take it in turns walking around the pot and dropping in their own little bit of food.

While the first beggar was walking around it suddenly occurred to him that if he kept his piece of meat no one would miss it out of so many bits of food and he could have it for breakfast. So instead of putting it in the pot he picked up a small stone off the floor of the hut and dropped it in with a loud plop so that the others would think it was the bit of meat. It was dark in the hut and he was sure no one would notice. Of course the second beggar had the same selfish idea, and the third and fourth. They all waited there in the dark for the supposed soup to cook, each thinking how they had easily conned each of the others and the fact that they would have their own extra bit of food for breakfast.

Of course when the soup was served all they had was a bowl of hot water each but they couldn't say anything could they? They all knew that they had tried to con each other. So they all went to sleep feeling very hungry.

This little story makes the point of the need to share very clear. Just like the beggar's soup – very clear! You can also read the Story of the Hungry Crowd from the *Children's Bible* (Lion Publishing).

There are lots of examples of sharing in the Bible, let's listen to this one where Jesus helps feed a crowd of 5,000 people.

This story could be called the miracle of sharing.

In the senior school some of the classes got together and decided so see what they could come up with once they put their heads together and decided to share their abilities. Class 1S produced a mosaic house. We made slides to show how various people shared their talents to help build it up.

Class 2S produced a stained glass window effect.

Class 3S managed to make a patchwork cushion. This was a highly skilled job and took a long time to make but working together with a little help from another teacher the final effect was achieved.

Here in the school we have tried sharing in a practical way to help the children in Queen Mary's Hospital. Over the past few weeks we have gathered together some toys and books that can be given to these children to help brighten Christmas day for them.

But the question remains, why do we share at this time of year? Well, this is the time of year when Christians celebrate the birth of Jesus. They believe that God gave his own son Jesus to guide and keep them on the right track through life.

20 Barriers (relationships and forgiveness) (upper)

Aims

(a)   to explore the use of artificial and natural barriers in the world
(b)   to appreciate how our relationships may be affected by the emotional barriers we erect from time to time

Method

1   Barriers in nature – e.g. hedgehog (spines), tortoise (shell), beavers (making a dam), and many others.

2   Artificial barriers – it could be a good idea to begin with a visit perhaps to a dam, if in London to the Thames Flood Barrier, or again to see some walls to keep people in or out. Walls or barriers can offer protection for those, and from those, inside or outside the barrier. Also there are other sorts of barriers – national boundaries, passports, even private conversations. It may be possible to show slides of the Berlin Wall, of the Great Wall of China, or Hadrian's Wall; some walls have escape stories connected with them. The Faith in Action series (RMEP) has *The Story of Brother Andrew* concerning smuggling Bibles into the Iron Curtain countries (another barrier).

3   Emotional barriers – we build them to protect our feelings, we have private conversations so we don't hurt other people or ourselves. Pupils may not tell their parents everything they do, e.g. when they get into trouble at school, etc. Sometimes a person (even a friend) offends us – a fight in the playground can mean we don't speak for days, perhaps we watch parents having an argument, perhaps we sulk because we can't have our own way (e.g. watching television).

4   Breaking down barriers – we say 'Hello' which can lead to the breaking down of barriers and the start of a new relationship. Now we build bridges, not walls or barriers – this can suggest *forgiveness*. One can use examples from the Bible – The Prodigal Son (Luke 15:11-32) is a good one because the father forgives but the older son doesn't appear to. This can be acted out and taken further than the parable, or reset as a young person running away from home. You could also use 'God is no Scrooge' by Flor McCarthy in *Veritas*.

Explore the idea of falling out with people and how one tries to restore good relationships. You could develop the theme of 'barriers and bridges' to include the notion of personal space.

5   Relationships need trust – again many religions are full of examples of trust where we rely upon people not to let us down: e.g.

David & Jonathan	(1 Samuel 19:1-7)
Moses	(Exodus Ch 3-4)
Elijah	(1 Kings 18:25-40)
Jesus	(Luke 12:22-31)
Rama & Sita etc.	J. E. Gray *Indian Tales and Legends* (OUP, 1979)
Guru Gobind Singh	*The Saint Soldier* (Sikh Missionary Society)

6   People we rely on – bus drivers and train drivers to get us to school and work. Sometimes we feel we can rely on strangers because they are distant from us, but often we share secrets with close friends and this can help us cement and develop our friendship. This sharing of our secrets is often the way many people pray, sharing with God their worries and successes, seeing him as a close friend.

21 The Good Samaritan (upper)

The class were aware of the relationship between Jews and Samaritans.

1   Show filmstrip – Japonica.

Read story of Good Samaritan from the Gospel of St. Luke (Luke 10:25-37), followed by class discussion and linking with filmstrip i.e. modern equivalents.

Class drama – acting of play of 'The Good Neighbour'. Children decide on story.

2 Play written up.

Acting out of newspaper reporter/TV reporter, reporting incident, interviewing, etc.

In groups of 4/5 write up story for paper, design newspaper headlines, type up stories.

Some examples of children's work:

16.1.87

Friday 13th

On Friday 13th January an old man called Big Bad Sam was badly beaten by a group of local thugs. He was found by 19-year-old John Smith and 18-year-old Tricia Collins on their way to Cinderella Night Club in Purley. John, a motor mechanic saw the old man lying on the ground and covered him with his coat, whilst Tricia summoned the police and ambulance. Police investigations have revealed that 3 persons saw the old man lying injured, but failed to report it.

(From Mirror reporter Fred Browning)

31.1.87

Everton

On Friday evening at 9.00 a 60-year-old man was beaten to the ground and kicked in the head. Police believe that thugs were responsible. They took all the old mans pension. A young couple, who were going to Bunny's Disco in Croydon were walking through the alley when they noticed him lying in a pool of blood. Tom Jones, a 23-year-old baker and his 22-year-old wife Katrina summoned the police. The police are now investigating the matter. They believe that 3 other people saw the old man and omitted to inform the police.

3.12.1987

Disco tragedy

On 3rd December 1987 a man was
badly beaten up in a spooky alley
police believe that 4 local youths
were involved they took all his
money and ran off Leaving him for
dead. He was found by Charlie
Brown a 16-year-old school boy and
15-year-old Tricia Bakes on their
way home from a school disco.
Whilst Charlie stayed with the man
Tricia went to phone the police and
ambulance. Police believe some
people may have seen the incident
but didn't report it.

11.1.87

Old man mugged!

Hallo, my name is Jane Max-
well. An old man was beaten
up in an alley his name was
called Dean Greenslade. He
is in a critical condition. A
couple of people were being
questioned.

14.12.87

Couple comes to the rescue

A young couple, on their way
home from the disco, walk
through the alley. They notice the
hurt man and rush over to help
him. The girl runs to phone the
police and ambulance, while the
boy comforts the old man by talking to him. He covers the old man
over with his jacket. Within
minutes the police and ambulance
arrive. The old man is taken to the
hospital. The police begin their
questioning.

02.11.87

The good neighbour

One winter evening the old
man was walking through
the badly lit ally when a gang
of thugs "jumped" him
knocked him to the ground,
kicked him in the head, and
then took all his pension
money. The gang then ran
away leaving the old man
lying in the pool of blood.

A little while later, two
women walk through the
alley on their way to the laun-
drette. They are busy gossip-
ing, notice the old man lying
down and they think he is
drunk. When they walk
away because they do not
want to become involved.
Then a drunk comes through
the alley, trips over the old
man, and then searches him
for money. He finds £1.00,
and walks off to buy more to
drink.

3   Whole class discussion/questioning of:

(a)   the people who 'walked on by' and did not stop to help and why they didn't stop, etc.

(b)   questioning four thugs who beat up old men – why they did what they did and the possible implications

4   Quick class play of 'Good Samaritan' from the Gospel of St. Luke – attempt to link that with class's modern equivalent.

The samples of the pupils' work make one wonder whether telling the Parable of the Good Samaritan had any relevance. The accounts make it clear that the pupils can relate their own scenario with little problem but there is no evidence of any reflection on theological issues. So where is the relevance of the story? Most pupils can create a modern equivalent of a sort, but none of the accounts acknowledge the outsider as the agent of the injured person's salvation. The gruesome story is attractive but little attention is paid either to the condition of the injured person or those who try to help.

Perhaps one is being too critical but there is a very good point hidden in this account about the telling and re-telling of Bible stories. To put the story in your own words is easily done, but if the purposes of the parable are ignored what is the value of the exercise? This particular parable was used again in discussion and one pupil volunteered the innkeeper as the most important person. By simply asking pupils to re-tell the story we do not encourage them to be incisive enough, we are not demanding enough and by not asking the correct question we do not help them to reflect upon the story they know. Children will think as deeply as adults about Bible stories but not necessarily of the same things – their vision can be more stimulating.

22   An approach to the Christmas story (upper)

Having looked through the many old Christmas cards in a classroom drawer and noted how many of them depicted angels we focused on the two birth narratives with the role of the angels very much in our minds.

As the group was relatively bright and interested I was able to explain that in the New Testament there were different 'books' written by different people and that two of these books had stories of the birth of Jesus. Joseph's side and the visit of the Wise Men were presented in St. Matthew and Mary's story was told in St. Luke.

We discussed the fact that almost all Jews wanted to get married and have a family and how sad people felt if they could not have children (referred to Samuel). The story of John the Baptist's parents (Luke 1:8) was told and then parts of the story were read. We discussed what an angel looked like and the class tried to draw one. We cut out old Christmas cards and stuck angels in our books.

We then went on to talk of the angels appearing to Mary, to Joseph, to the shepherds and to the Wise Men. The children realised that it did not really matter what an angel looked like, but that the important fact was that an angel is a messenger from God.

This little play was the result.

It was 'made-up' with help from *The Good News Bible*. Narrator's speeches by teacher and children – otherwise children's own thoughts/words. 5/6 sessions. Bible nearby to begin with and then referred to when children 'dried-up'. All children involved and enjoyed the sessions. Nine very out-going children.

Angel:	Peace be with you, Mary. God is with you. Don't be frightened Mary. You will have a baby boy and you must call the baby Jesus.
Mary:	How can I have a baby. I'm not married yet.
Angel:	God's holy spirit will shine on you and the baby Jesus will be called the Son of God.
Mary:	I will do what God wants.
	(*Joseph goes to see Mary and knocks at the door.*)
Mary:	Come in. Hello Joseph.
Joseph:	Hello Mary. How are you?
Mary:	I've got something to tell you.
Joseph:	Come on then, tell me.
Mary:	An angel came and said that I'm going to have a baby boy and I must call him Jesus.
Joseph:	What? Say that again! You must be kidding.
Mary:	No I'm not kidding.
Joseph:	You must be, 'cause we're not married yet.
Mary:	An angel did come to me with a message from God. Baby Jesus will be God's son.

Joseph:	I'll have to go home and think about this.
	(*Joseph goes to see his friend Peter.*)
Joseph:	Hello Peter.
Peter:	Hello Joseph.
Joseph:	I've got a problem. Mary says she is having a baby and we're not even married yet – and I don't know what to do.
Peter:	What does Mary say about it all?
Joseph:	She said to me – an angel appeared and the angel said she was going to have a baby and the baby's got to be named Jesus and it's going to be God's son.
Peter:	I'd chuck her.
Joseph:	I can't. She's going to have a baby and needs someone to look after her.
Peter:	Well, I wouldn't marry her.
	(*Joseph goes*)
Joseph:	Goodbye, Peter.
Peter:	Goodbye Joseph.
	(*Joseph goes to bed and while he is asleep an angel appears.*)
Angel:	Joseph.
Joseph:	Who's that?
Angel:	Joseph.
Joseph:	Who are you?
Angel:	I'm an angel from God. I've come to give you a message from God.
Joseph:	What is this message?
Angel:	You must marry Mary. The baby will be God's son.
Joseph:	Strange.
Angel:	You must look after her.
Joseph:	I'll do as God says.
	(*He goes back to sleep.*)

Some time afterwards the Romans told everyone they had to go back to where they had been born to be registered.

Joseph had been born in Bethlehem, so he and Mary had to go on a long journey. Bethlehem was full. Lots of other people had to be registered too.

Joseph:	Come on Mary. Not far to go now.
Mary:	I'm very tired.
Joseph:	Let's try at this inn.
	(*He knocks.*)
Innkeeper:	What can I do for you?
Joseph:	Have you got anywhere for us to stay?
Innkeeper:	No I'm full up.
Joseph:	Never mind, Mary. We'll find somewhere else.
Mary:	I hope so.
Joseph:	Here's another inn.
	(*He knocks.*)
Innkeeper:	Yes. What do you want?
Joseph:	Is there any room for us in your inn?
Innkeeper:	No, because it's all full up.
Joseph:	We'll have to find another inn. Don't worry. I'll find somewhere.
	(*He knocks at another door.*)
Innkeeper:	What do you want?
Joseph:	Have you anywhere for us to stay?
Innkeeper:	No, sorry, we're full up.
Joseph:	We're desperate. My wife's having a baby.
Innkeeper's wife:	You can sleep in our stable.
Joseph:	It's better than nothing.
Wife:	We will give you clean straw for you to sleep on. And you can put the baby in the soft hay in the manger. Come this way. There you are.

Mary rested in the stable. That night baby Jesus was born. Mary wrapped him in strips of cloth and laid him in the manger to sleep.

In the fields outside Bethlehem were some shepherds guarding their sheep. Some were asleep.

Suddenly there was a bright light in the sky. The shepherds were frightened.

Angel:	Don't be afraid. I bring good news. A baby is born in Bethlehem. He is God's son, your saviour – Christ the Lord. You will find him in a stable wrapped in strips of cloth and lying in a manger.
Angels:	Glory to God and Peace on earth.
Shepherds:	Let's go to Bethlehem to find the baby.

So they hurried off and found Mary and Joseph and saw the baby lying in the manger.

All: Away in a manger . . .
(*Shepherds kneeling by baby.*)

23 Helping (1)

Aim	To make children aware of: (a) help received (b) helping others
Focal point	Visitor e.g. policeman.
Materials required	Paintings, or pictures showing people who can help us.
Preparation	(a) paintings of lollipop lady, police officer, nurse, dinner staff, welfare workers. (b) dramatic scene – children falling, helping to dress (c) song 'We can help each other all day long' (Joyful Songs, Oliver and Boyd, 1979)

Development

Teacher –	greeting, suggestions from children about helpers, show and talk about paintings.
Drama –	group of children.
Song –	as above.
Teacher –	ways in which we help at home. ways in which young people in religious traditions help at home. a Festival is coming – how can we help?
Prayer –	made up by child.

23   Helping (2)

Aim	To help children to become aware of the need to give and receive help.
Focal point	A family (visitors to assembly) or members of different families from different countries.
Materials required	Domestic items.
Preparation	(a) paintings of different members of family helping each other (b) poem or story about family (c) songs 'This is the way we . . .' (tune 'Here we go round the Mulberry Bush')
Development of Assembly	
Teacher –	introduce visitors – why they are here – thanks for helping with assembly. how they help in their family: Grandma may baby-sit Auntie may take the children out Daddy/uncle may read to them
Teacher –	family life – its importance in religious life e.g. Jesus, Moses, Muhammed etc. and their families – what life was like – how they could have helped each other. children's own thoughts – thanking for families and helping each other.

24 Helping others

Focal point	A cook and an empty table.
Music	Taped music.
Materials	Sacks, meal's ingredients – tins and raw vegetables, table setting, plates etc.
Development	Ingredients in today's lunch.
Bible Story	Read the Feeding of the Five Thousand. (Mark 6:37–44) Boy's view.
Asking questions	Children ask questions of cook, importance of food in some religions, people who do not eat certain kinds of food.
Song	'Super Supper March' (*Tinder Box Assembly Book*, Black, 1982)
Taped music	For exit. Further extensions – children's cooking and development, foods etc.

25 Friends (1)

Awe and wonder

Participation in festivals,
  games and sports
Presents, prizes, winning and
  losing
Excitement
Enjoyment of play
Unhappiness, fear, hatred
Concern, happiness

Relationships

My friends, friends at school
  at home, clubs and societies
What is a friend? Loyalty
Common ideas and friction
Visiting others' homes, birthday
  parties, other celebrations
Soured friendship
My family, my church, mosque, or
  temple

Other people

David and Jonathan (Samuel
  Ch 18:1–5)
Ruth and Naomi (Ruth Ch 1)
The Good Samaritan
  (Luke Ch 10:25)
The Prodigal Son (Luke
  Ch 15:11–32)
A doctor, police constable, lollipop
  lady, nurse, teacher
Buddha and Ananda

Friends

Skills

Art work, painting,
  drawing, collage,
  modelmaking
A play, class
  assembly, pantomimes
Drama and music

Belief and practices

Harvest
  celebrations
Christmas
Epiphany
Diwali
Eid–ul–Adha
Whitsun
Easter
} a time for friends to
celebrate together,
giving and
sharing, and
remembering

Passover – the sharing of a meal

25 Friends (2)

Awe and wonder

Sun, seasons
Pets, helpful animals

Relationships

Relatives, first friends –
  neighbours, playgroups
What is a friend?
Interests, hobbies
People who care for us –
  police etc.
Helping sick

Friends

Other people

People in history who helped others –
  Eric Liddell, Edith Cavell, Florence
  Nightingale
Acts of bravery in history – Captain Oates
Stories – Lion and Mouse,
Queen Bee

Skills

Painting – portraits
Things we do together:
  Movement – pairs, moving together
  Situations – helping/saving friends
  Three-legged and wheel-barrow races
Poems/creative writing
Songs and rhymes

Belief and practices

Christmas, gifts, Easter,
  Passover, Diwali, Baisakhi,
  Eid-ul-Adha, Birthday of Guru
  Nanak

25 Friends (3)

Awe and wonder

Special friends
Games
Enduring friends

Relationships

Our friends can be:
Helpful – Krishna and Arjuna
An example – Elisha to Elijah,
   Abraham and Lot
Loyal – Naomi and Ruth, Rama and
   Sita
Forgiving – Jesus and Peter,
   Zaccheus
Charity – Save the Children, Red
   Cross, Red Crescent
Chains of friendship – local and
   world wide

Friends

Skills

Drama
Art
Music
   Look out for loneliness
   Would you walk on the
   other side?
   There are hundreds and
   thousands of . . .

Beliefs and practices

Friends in places of worship
Harvest festivals, sharing
   festivals and major celebrations
Birthdays and special days

Here are some further ideas of themes to be developed:

26 Obedience

Law keeping – for the good of society
Keeping the rules of the school
Obeying our parents
Adam and Eve (Genesis Ch 3)
Soldiers – obeying commands
Pets – teaching them to be obedient
Ten Commandments (Exodus Ch 20:1-17)
Rules of the Road – as a motorist
as a pedestrian

A necessary part of life?

27 Elements – earth, air, fire, water

Aim – Awareness of the world around us

Earth – Genesis (as in the fields)
Parable of the Sower (Mark 4:3-8)
Growing things
Springtime and harvest
Uses, need

Air – need

Water – Moses in the Bullrushes (Exodus 1:1-2, 10)
The sea
Rain
Uses, need

Fire – Moses & the Burning Bush (Exodus 3:1-6)
Uses (heat, light), dangers, need

The above theme could be expressed through writing, drawing, painting, dance and drama, music and singing.

28 Sight

Sight – I can see
Blind people – braille, guide dogs
Glasses – magnification
Music
Television
Colours
Reading

29 Hearing

Hearing – I can hear
Isolating sounds
Voices – animal sounds
The wind
Noise
Radio
Deafness
Music – instruments

Key issues for the secondary school teacher

The greatest concern for material for teaching the pupil with learning difficulties probably comes from the secondary school teacher. The problems that exist in the primary, middle and the special schools are intensified because of the nature of the curriculum, the system of staffing, timetabling and so on. It seems easier to the secondary school teacher to deal with the slow learner in the middle or primary school where one teacher is largely responsible for all the activities within the classroom. But the grass always looks greener on the other side of the fence. Most secondary schools can call upon a range of resources far beyond the smaller school. However, there are particular difficulties with which the secondary school teacher has to wrestle which arise out of policy decisions made within each school.

This chapter will consider some of the policies, looking at their effect on the classroom teacher, the pupil, and the environment in which learning takes place. It will conclude by looking at some teaching methods which may be adopted in the classroom, particularly considering the use of resources.

Curriculum policy

So much has been written on this that it is impossible to know where to begin; there seems to be a plethora of teachers and administrators with qualifications in Curriculum Development to such an extent that one wonders who is left to do the teaching. It can be quite difficult for the assistant teacher to have a say in curriculum policy, or at least a say that is listened to, and how often do the designers of the curriculum pay attention to the pupils? As one visits a number of secondary schools one can appreciate the diversity of approach, some appear to run on the same lines as they did thirty years ago, others have made radical changes and review the situation regularly.

The fundamental question in relation to this book is: 'For whom is the curriculum designed?' This may appear to be a very obvious question but if one begins from the premise that the pupils are the centre, the focus, of all educational activity, then presumably the curriculum will be designed for their benefit. Should one agree with this? If so then the next question is: 'Which pupils will be given particular consideration within the curriculum?' Pupils tend not to be the same. They are, happily, people with a whole range of personalities, ideas and abilities, so how can any school with between say 800 and 2,500 pupils recognise and meet these requirements? Ideally all educators would surely like to meet the individual needs of every pupil but that does not appear possible at the moment. So where do the curriculum planners draw the line?

There are a number of pressures on such people – teachers and pupils, of course, but also governors, parents, local authorities and central government. Pupils who represent perhaps one in six of the total school population will not be an immediate pressure upon the planner. The slow learner has to take a place in the queue, but the queue is likely to be long and the needs of the vast majority can be paramount.

For most people with an interest in secondary school education the examination system has an overriding importance. Motivation for many pupils is provided by the race to acquire high marks in external examinations. In addition, what is taught in the years before the two-year external examination course is largely determined by those examinations themselves. So the curriculum can be a response to a vast number of external factors not the least of which is an external examination.

At the time of writing, the new 16+ GCSE examinations have not yet been taken, but the 'O' level and CSE examinations did not account for many of the pupils for whom teachers need specific advice and resources. Although many secondary schools entered every pupil for a CSE course, in fact a sizeable minority never completed the course. Whether the situation will be repeated with the GCSE remains to be seen but it is at least a possibility.

All this has a dramatic effect on the curriculum requirements of pupils with learning difficulties. Is the curriculum policy in the secondary school determined by the academic requirements of the top 20% of pupils, the average or the bottom 15 to 20%? Certainly the policy-makers wish to ensure that every pupil, regardless of ability, receives the best possible deal but like all policy-makers they have priorities. It seems that teachers of children with learning difficulties in secondary schools will never be able to get to grips with the real issues until these pupils are given priority. Unless curriculum planners sit down to decide first and foremost what is best for the slow learner, these pupils will always be expected to learn by means of a system which is not geared to their requirements.

Each teacher of RE or any other subject has to come to terms with curriculum policy before they can begin to think about teaching strategies, methods and resources. But, however good a teacher may be and whatever resources are to hand, there is no possibility of fully meeting the needs of the pupil with learning difficulties unless curriculum policy gives them a higher priority than is normal in the secondary school.

Timetabling

For the assistant teacher in any secondary school the issue of power can be crucial. To whom does one turn to get things changed? Well it depends, of course, on the change required but there can be no doubt that the teacher who controls the timetable is someone to cultivate. Schools vary but *most* secondary schools have periods of about 40 minutes, though in some cases and for some subjects two periods can be placed together. Teacher attitudes can vary over whether they wish to teach mixed ability classes for 40 or 80 minutes, but the work done in the middle schools on this project suggests that an 80 minute block opens up far more possibilities to both pupil and teacher. The longer period makes for greater flexibility if required (it may not be).

As far as the RE teacher is concerned the first battle is to ensure that the subject is properly timetabled. There is little excuse for any secondary school not timetabling two periods of RE per week in the first three years, or up to the beginning of the external examination syllabus. If it *is* the case that two periods per week are allocated to RE, then the teacher has to decide whether the time could more effectively be spent on two separate periods or one double period. Again the timetabler's support is required, but teachers have negotiated with colleagues after the timetable has been drawn up in order to allow themselves a block period.

Similarly schools where there is only one period per week of RE have again created some flexibility by allowing, for example, two periods per week of RE for the first half of the year and then none for the rest. The onus falls on the RE teacher to decide what is best for them and for the pupils. Clearly the type of timetabling could have an effect on teaching methods or vice versa. In one secondary school a year group was timetabled for a double period of RE at the end of the afternoon which made trips to the locality more straightforward.

The experience of visiting many schools and working quite intensively in some of them shows that the RE teacher has to come up with a blueprint of what is required, a long term project over say five years, which lays down clearly and succinctly the requirements of the subject and the particular benefits that will accrue to pupils of different abilities. This incorporates far more than the timetable, but it is a crucial element in the planning of how best to respond to the needs of pupils with learning difficulties.

Aims and objectives

Having fought the curriculum and timetabling battles one is now left to survey how the week of teaching looks. It is time to set down aims and objectives. Given the task of teaching RE to the slow learner it appears that successful teaching involves clarity. The pupil should know exactly what is required by the teacher and the teacher, too, should know exactly what he or she requires of the pupil.

Most teachers will set down their aims and objectives when planning lessons or schemes of work; when teaching slow learners it is very helpful to set down staged objectives. This enables the teacher to set goals which can be achieved by the pupil and that achievement recognised and approved of by both of them. The key element in this is for the pupil to experience success: he or she has done what was asked, done it well, can receive praise and encouragement and then move on to the next assignment. It can be tiresome and frustrating to plan work in such detail, but it does seem from teaching slow learners that the greater the planning, the more meticulous the staged objectives, the more benefit there is to the pupil and therefore the teacher.

Is it possible to draw up different sets of objectives for each pupil or for small groups of pupils with learning difficulties so that the teacher becomes more sensitive to their special requirements? If this breaks down the teacher's image of the 'average' pupil, then the change in attitude will benefit all involved. In the project work teaching appeared easier, more relaxed, with the pupils responding more purposefully because they knew what was required, they grew to recognise that each lesson was in a sense tailormade for them. In the same way that the GCSE expects a hierarchy of skills to be demonstrated, so each programme of work can be designed to demonstrate a similar hierarchy.

This implies that, once the content is decided in broad terms, the teaching strategy is crucial. In my opinion content is of only secondary importance. Many secondary school teachers do appear to be more concerned with the content of what is taught than the method of teaching it. Perhaps it is a legacy of their own subject specialism or perhaps it is due to the lack of scope offered within the constraints of the average secondary school. Content *is* important, but if it is so important then the vehicle of its transmission must be crucial.

Assessment and examinations

How effectively have any of us as teachers assessed the achievements of our pupils? Perhaps it will be helpful if I take some personal examples. My own school reports, from a grammar school in South Wales, are largely made up of the one liner – sometimes a sentence but more often a 'good', 'quite good' or 'slipshod'. It did seem a little thin for a term's work, yet when I started teaching myself I realised the enormity of the task. At my second school I taught everyone and succumbed to the temptation of writing 'satisfactory' on more reports than I care to admit. It was simply a matter of time and space, and I suppose the 'satisfactory' for RE didn't shatter the parents' world too much. Looking back I suspect it meant the pupil didn't work too hard or too little, behaved within the limits of tolerance and made a sporadic contribution to the lesson. The one major advantage that I did have at the school was that I actually knew every pupil, something few others did, so when a pupil was being discussed I was able to make some sort of contribution.

If this sounds jaded, careless or even slightly flippant, I would offer in defence my two children's school reports from their comprehensive school. These consist of grades for achievement and effort – no words, just a list of grades from A to E. Parents' evenings can be a surprise too. Parents have been known to listen open-mouthed as the comments from one or two teachers did not fit their clutched piece of paper, only to discover they were talking about someone else's child! All parents and teachers can see this – as parents we want better patterns of assessment for our children yet it is difficult as teachers to provide full assessment profiles for pupils. Sheer weight of numbers makes this extremely time-consuming and takes a lot of energy.

However, this project suggested that schools can rub salt in the wounds of the slow learner. Speech Days often celebrate achievement and rightly so, but should a wake celebrate the relative failures? So much of the recognition of achievement rests upon the twin skills of reading and writing, particularly in the secondary school. Teachers who work with pupils in primary and/or middle schools can often recognise ability within a pupil because they spend more time with them, using a variety of teaching strategies, but the pile of exercise books to be marked takes its own toll in the secondary school.

Perhaps this is too bleak a picture, it certainly is in some schools where great efforts have been made to give credit for particular aspects of the pupils' work. A willingness to discuss, a skill with the paintbrush, in sculpture or dance are so important if the pupil is to feel a sense of worth. Time and time again in the schooling of pupils with learning difficulties it is clear that one block of learning is the expected sense of failure and the worthlessness of what is produced.

Another anecdote may focus this more clearly on Religious Education. A teacher said to me some time ago that one of his pupils didn't do much and was a bit 'slow' in fact, then the class visited the local church and the pupil's work blossomed. 'He did so well and he found such a spiritual insight, I gave him 7 on 10' the teacher said. Part of me found this very worthy, though I hope the teacher realised that his problems were just beginning because if the pupil could achieve 7 on 10 on one topic then surely, correctly motivated, he could do it again or even better. Part of me twitched because I wondered how any of us mark or assess spirituality. I have a nightmare of Ezekiel handing me a written version of his vision and me marking it and handing it back with 'fanciful' written on it, or 'imaginative but lacks clarity'. And as for the Book of Revelation . . . So I felt the teacher was making assumptions about the pupil and about religion which needed more consideration than merely handing out 7 on 10.

Clearly what we as teachers assess must be related to the objectives and again clear, staged objectives appear to be the most effective method of assessing a slow learner's progress. They also mean that the pupil can recognise progress and respond to it. It may be that the development of school profiles over the next ten years or so will help the pupil with learning problems to see these in a broader and more comforting perspective. It could also offer some comfort to anxious parents who find it hard to recognise how their son or daughter is benefiting from attending school.

Examinations are a different and more precise issue. The most significant issue concerning them in the secondary school is the way they have a direct effect upon the type of work and the method of teaching done in the pre-external examination years. The pupil who has learning difficulties will always be at a disadvantage in this situation because:

(a) the ability to read and write is crucial of course
(b) some pupils 'know' what is required but simply are not able to articulate it
(c) the lack of confidence developed over a number of years makes it extremely difficult to overcome inhibitions
(d) the methods used to teach them may not correspond to the methods required to pass examinations

The attempt at the middle school to provide a different sort of examination is laudable. It would not help a pupil directly to pass an examination at 16+, however it might encourage secondary schools to experiment with examination techniques in the lower school with a long term view of eventually supplementing the written forms of examination still prevalent in GCSE. Incidentally, it is often forgotten that the popularity of the project-style examination can mean the pupil with learning difficulties has to complete perhaps six or eight long term projects, whereas the more able pupil has only to complete a written paper of $1\frac{1}{2}$ to 2 hours.

In Religious Studies, while the examiner does wish to test knowledge, it is more difficult to examine understanding particularly with pupils who do not take to reading and writing. The aspect of experience is a key one in religion and it would be unfortunate if there were no way of enabling the pupil to express that experience. If one considers the phenomena of religion it is obvious that art, ritual and music all play a profound part in expressing the force of religious experience, yet the temptation is to test a pupil's understanding through literacy only. This was illustrated most clearly above where the pupil who identified the most important person in the Parable of the Good Samaritan as the innkeeper would have been corrected by a secondary school RE specialist because the answer did not conform to the accepted tradition. One should not argue a general case from a particular incident, but secondary school teachers may allow their subject specialism to blur what can only be termed as a genuine moment of insight.

Oral examinations have become more common, though they still carry a fairly small allocation of marks. This could be a very important area for Religious Studies to supplement the other skills tested. It is of course difficult but to engage a pupil in a discussion of a text, an artefact or a short piece of video should be able to demonstrate far more of their insight, sensitivity and awareness than a written paper.

Value, relevance and content

In the 1960s and 1970s there was a greater emphasis in some areas of education on relevance. It may appear to be a parody but the argument was that, if pupils in the secondary school were to be easily motivated, then a key factor in this motivation was relevance. The syllabus had to be relevant to the life and experience of the pupils. This was reflected to a considerable extent in RE through the work of Harold Loukes and the influential RE syllabus of the West Riding in the mid-1960s. So influential was this that the syllabuses of the 1980s still reflect the notion of relevance in their suggestions for years four and five. This is often cloaked in the guise of sex, drugs, euthanasia and other social problems. My own view is that this is often the least satisfactory aspect of RE teaching in the secondary school. However, that is another subject.

The successful teaching observed at all levels of schooling appeared to rely less on relevance and more on good teaching, well-planned and prepared lessons. The social issues so popular in the secondary school can be just as far removed from the pupil's experience as any other aspect of the syllabus. Some pupils guard their private lives very carefully – from both parents and school. It cannot be assumed that the totality of the pupil's experience finds expression in school.

Surely motivation, particularly for the slow learner, may be provided more effectively by praise and acknowledgement of the pupil's work. There are many classroom activities which are enjoyable, lend themselves to stimulating and interesting lessons, but are not directly relevant to the world of the pupil outside school. The major argument must be that the process of learning is of prime importance because it passes on to the slow learner a method, or number of methods of learning which can be applied in other areas and in later life.

The application of the term 'relevance' has more point if the activity or lesson being taught can be recognised as having value. It is something worth doing perhaps because of the end-product, perhaps because of the learning method, perhaps simply because it is enjoyable. So relevance is less related to the experiences of the pupil outside school and much more to the value of learning processes: relevance becomes a more important feature of education if it is interpreted in this way.

However, it is important also to reflect on content and the relationship between content, value and relevance. Many RE teachers have to battle with the expectations of the pupil; if a topic is not overtly and obviously religious then in the eyes of the pupil it may not be RE. This, in turn, means the pupil may respond quite differently from when the topic has a clearly defined religious focus. So content has an importance which must not be undervalued, but the content should be selected by the teacher and not by the pupil, or by what the teacher believes the pupil will respond to most easily. This sounds a little confusing but it does appear to be extremely important when teaching RE to the slow learner because it is closely linked to the clarity of aims and objectives.

An RE syllabus has, one hopes, religion at its centre, it also should have a teacher who is able to teach it. Most Agreed Syllabuses of the 1970s and 1980s are very flexible, allowing the secondary specialist the freedom to develop their own particular syllabus to fit the experience and expertise within their school. So the content of a particular school's syllabus has to be related to what can be taught with available resources. It can be a fruitless task to try to decide what the pupils *need* to know and then to construct a syllabus around it – relevance in this situation is not only not possible, it is undesirable. This is the sense in which content is considered to be of lesser importance than the process by which pupils learn. The content of RE varies from secondary school to secondary school regardless of any Agreed Syllabus; there appears to be no universal core in RE content, though most secondary schools do still concentrate on the Bible and/or the life of Jesus for some of the time.

When teaching pupils with learning difficulties of any sort the teacher has to remember that the details of content are unlikely to be remembered for any length of time. This is quite possibly true of all of us. Having met former students some years after their teacher-training, I found they all remembered their field courses in Iona, Taize or Coventry but few, I'm afraid, appeared to remember my lectures. Still it is a point many of us fail to recognise in our lesson plans. Do we want the pupils to 'know' a particular piece of information? Is it crucial? It may be that from time to time it is considered important that pupils *do* learn a piece of scripture or a series of statements of belief, but some attention has to be given to the reason why it is being learned and how it will be learned.

In essence there has to be a balance between a content that is overtly to do with religion, and a method or strategy that makes the content interesting and relevant in the sense of 'value' to the pupil. This does raise a quite fundamental issue about the purpose of teaching. Is it to transmit information, to hand on the wisdom of the past that society considers important? Or is it to enable the pupil to develop skills, concepts and attitudes that will help him or her to fulfil their inner potential to the utmost degree? I believe that the answer is not either/or but both/and. As usual with such questions the answer lies in both camps, particularly so in RE where the dilemma of the educator in the secondary school is also the dilemma of the religions themselves. Do they seek to pass on received wisdom to the unquestioning young, or do they encourage the young to discover the religious truth for themselves? In effect virtually every religious group either directly or indirectly does both, though a particular religion may lean more to one aspect than another.

This is one reason why the issue of content and method is so crucial in RE – it is crucial in religion itself. Try looking back over your own religious education. What did you learn at school? How was it taught? Where did the school assembly fit into the pattern? If you were brought up in whole or partly in a religious tradition what was taught? How was it taught? In my own experience of primary and secondary education in the 1950s and early 1960s there was little difference between learning one's tables by rote and learning the Lord's Prayer and the Nicene Creed. They were learned because it was required – understanding the various concepts and vocabulary was considered unimportant. And yet, years later the maths tables stick in my mind as does the Creed, so the process of learning by rote in this case might be said to have provided a reservoir that could be tapped in later life when given greater maturity and experience.

Diagnosis

Earlier in this book attention was drawn to the problem of diagnosis. Teachers, or rather some of them, are not trained to diagnose reasons for apparent inability to learn, and some learning problems are extremely difficult for even the expert to diagnose let alone cure. In the secondary school the RE teacher may teach over 400 pupils per week, in some schools it may even be over 600. The chances of picking out particular learning difficulties and responding to them are remote simply because of weight of numbers and the time allocation of lessons. So teachers generally should absolve themselves of the guilt of being unable to diagnose, particularly in the secondary school.

However, as is the case in life, the issue is not quite so clear cut. The pupil who does not achieve as one expects *may* have a learning difficulty but they may also not be responding to a particular teacher. Most people have a problem of learning at something or other, perhaps not reading but driving or any other skill. Most teacher assessments of pupils are based on the values of society and this can be reflected in how a particular teacher responds to a particular pupil. As teachers we often wish to see in our pupils the reflection of our own values and it can be difficult to create empathy with a pupil who has a problem we do not share and have not shared.

Teachers in secondary schools are often conscious of the pace at which they need to go – this book has to be finished this term, the class has to have finished the Tudors by the summer holiday. The problem of content means that the syllabus can be overloaded and there is little time to pay attention to the answer that isn't the expected one. This has been referred to earlier as dissonance i.e. the answer to a question or a comment that comes at right-angles to what is expected or required. To explore why that answer arose or how it seemed correct can involve precious time; it is easier to dismiss it and pass on till one arrives at the answer one is seeking. Again the teacher runs the risk of only responding to what his or her requirements are, the teaching is being geared to the teacher and not to the requirements of the pupil.

Ironically in Religious Education there is a pattern to follow, for it is arguable that many of the great religious teachers posed questions that demanded reflection. They asked for time so that what they taught could be mulled over, discussed and then the conversation could move on. Indeed many of their actions invited comment and discussion. In other words one of the most common processes in the great religious teachers is to pose questions and challenge accepted orthodoxy. Rather than dismiss the element of dissonance they appear to look for it, to encourage it, for it breaks the mould of convention. Again religion and education could have a parallel concern, not one perhaps to be over-emphasised but one to be borne in mind. It is another example of how in teaching religion the teacher might well teach pupils of all abilities more effectively by looking closely at the teaching methods of those they teach about.

Status

With regard to status the RE teacher should have a sneaking sympathy with the pupil who has learning problems. It is extremely difficult for the slow learner to develop a sense of worth in the school whatever label is attached to the learning difficulties. It is very difficult to learn or to take an interest if one constantly feels undervalued or insignificant. Much of the work done in this project has re-emphasised the unoriginal but often overlooked conclusion that, if pupils are to learn more effectively, they must feel a personal sense of worth and value. This must be constantly reinforced as must their status as people and their achievements.

How like the RE teacher this can sound! How many RE teachers struggle along alone in their school feeling undervalued? How many have to argue for even minimally adequate timetabling and capitation? Does the school have a qualified RE specialist? Does that specialist have a room or does he or she tramp the corridors like the children of Israel in the wilderness? One could continue but if *any* teacher in the secondary school knows about lack of status and professional recognition then the RE teacher must be high on the list.

The RE teacher should not be professionally or morally *more* concerned about the slow learner than the teacher of any other subject – all teachers should be concerned. But they might find some element of common ground in the situation, for it is desperately difficult to maintain high professional standards if you feel colleagues do not accord you the status you expect.

Failure

Most of us would admit to failure in something in our lives, some of us may even feel we had experienced it more than we would wish. It is actually quite helpful for teachers with pupils who have learning problems to control their own guilt at failure. This is no copper-bottomed answer to the teaching of the slow learning pupil. Diagnosis is difficult, the reasons are multifarious and every teacher will experience failure. It seems to be an important feature of this project that failure has to be recognised – we expected too much of the pupils, didn't prepare adequately, couldn't respond when the pupils didn't understand etc. Surely, however, the great skill of teaching is to try a variety of approaches. There has to be a search to find a method which will induce a positive response. This will mean grasping the nettle and trying new approaches in the classroom, perhaps it will mean noise and possibly on occasions lack of control. 'Chalk and talk' is still popular, but it may help to split the class up into groups, encourage mini-discussions and anything which offers variety and the possibility of a different response.

It does require a great deal of courage to change one's teaching style and teachers know that if they do change (a) pupils may not respond as expected and (b) they may feel a lack of confidence. This is true, of course, but if teachers do not persist and at least try for some time then they are being as despondent as those they seek to help, and they do influence pupils by their attitude.

Base-line content

Finally, it seems that in mixed ability groups it is not helpful simply to grade the work and hand out different work to pupils of different ability. It is far more worthwhile if all pupils can begin at the same point and then develop as their ability allows. This will be in contradiction to many teachers who tend to select what should be achieved by the most able and then lower their sight for the lesser mortals. The suggestion here is that the teacher should begin by carrying *all* the pupils. Regardless of ability they start at the same point but there are springboards so that as the topic unfolds the most able can be given a particular route and the slow learner another more appropriate route, but they have both started together.

This approach raises problems across the curriculum for it implies that when creating a syllabus and certainly when planning a lesson, priority is given to the pupil with learning problems. It is no longer assumed that they can be 'fitted in' to the rest of the class but *their* concerns are considered first. This is not easy and it does have implications for resourcing, timetabling and lesson–planning, and perhaps most important of all it does mean that the teacher must be very clear about his or her aims and objectives.

Conclusion

It is difficult to draw any conclusions from such a diverse collection though some issues emerge very clearly. We appear to live in a society which looks for answers rather than deeper questions, all of us would like the quick tips which would help solve our immediate problem. Teachers' in-service courses are full of people who would really like the answer to the slow learner, morning assembly, pastoral care and so on, yet we know as teachers that very little of what we hear remains with us for any length of time. I can feel a sense of achievement if I have remembered and acted upon one idea from an in-service course a year later, but perhaps I just have a low threshold of achievement. One of the most satisfying moments came on a DES short course in Reading where about fifty teachers shared in a simulation of the Passover Meal. By the time the following Easter holidays arrived four had held a simulation in their classroom and were enthusiastic about it because of the enjoyment and learning that took place. Is four out of fifty a good average or not? In my estimation it is but then perhaps I should have higher expectations.

The example of the simulated Seder or Passover provide some insight into the response of the slow learner in RE. It involves a lot of preliminary work: the meal is to be prepared, the Seder dish properly laid out, each pupil given a copy of the Seder service, and wine and water and herbs and eggs to be arranged, yet it can be a wonderful occasion, to eat together in school, to live out symbolically one of the seminal events of Judaism. It involves little intellectual application and yet there is an enormous amount to be gained from this one event, not only about Jews but about symbol-ism, friendship, ritual and celebration. Such simulations, as long as they are not offensive to the religion concerned, can be a prime source for teaching RE to the pupil with learning difficulties. They need preparation, planning and are time-consuming, though given these they are very successful.

Certainly the clearest point that one has constantly met in this project is that teachers must be clear about their aims and objectives. Of course this is true for teachers of all ability groups but it is particularly important for the teacher of the slow learner. The clarity is passed on to the pupil and indeed it is helpful if the pupil can see exactly *what* is to be done, *why* it should be done and *where* it should be done. If the pupil shares in defining the objectives of a particular piece of work then that is an important educational exercise in itself, one which the pupil can apply to other areas of life.

Developing from this is the importance of staged objectives which mean that the teacher has a particular plan for each pupil or group of pupils. Their progress is easy to measure and both teacher and pupils can recognise progress and achievement. If there is one area which is crucial it is this one. Virtually all teachers acknowledge the importance of aims and objectives though they may not write them out for each topic or lesson (unfortunately). Staged objectives however define the pupils' progress very precisely and, while they may be of particular use in the special school, they would be most appropriate in the secondary classroom. If the teacher is to begin with a common content in the mixed ability classroom then a series of staged objectives makes the progression and the progress clear to each pupil. Some pupils will not progress very far or very rapidly, it is true, but in any class pupils quickly recognise the pecking order of ability in various subjects so the creation of a positive atmosphere is extremely important.

These two aspects join to the notion that pupils should develop a positive approach to the value of their own learning. This should not be confused with the teacher's assessment of them. They should ideally feel that *what* they learn has a value, not merely a relevance, and *how* they learn has a purpose. This should not be confused with the search for relevance. In this case the pupil will be able to recognise that he or she has learned a new skill. Learning will be measured by the pupil, not by the teacher; it will be a recognition of achievement. This would seem to me to be a development in educational terms of what all of us believe to be so important in life. We look for things we can measure against ourself – if we are convalescing it is an achievement to walk a little further, to run a little faster, to show more patience. All these things and many more have a value to each person, so it is hardly surprising that the slow learner should appreciate the value of his or her own worth. A sense of achievement however small is more than a step along the road, it is a recognition of the value of oneself, an identification of inner potential.

Self-assessment is an important aspect of education not least among pupils with learning difficulties who have to come to terms with the fact that school reports are written by a teacher and examinations have a faceless quality about them. So much of these pupils' learning hangs on the close personal relationship built up between themselves and the teacher that it is difficult to appreciate the impersonal nature of the examination system. It is more important to acknowledge this for the pupil whose learning has been so intensely personal. Is there a case for school reports or school profiles to contain the pupils' own reflections on how effectively they worked, what they achieved, what they found most difficult? In talking with many teachers who work with remedial pupils or teach in special schools it becomes clear that these pupils are people too. We can easily dismiss their opinions and deny them the self-respect and the fundamental human rights we afford to other 'brighter' pupils. And in doing this we rub more salt into the wound and continue the vicious circle of low expectation.

How effective are our assessment procedures in schools? As discussed above they seem to be very sketchy in some schools, they hardly provide a full profile of the pupils' progress across the board, nor do many appear to refer to the pupils' life outside school. What does a pupil's membership of Guides, Scouts or a Youth Club bring to the school? Does the pupil who has problems writing keep a diary at home? What books do they read and what television programmes do they watch? The assessments at school do not make up the whole person, they reflect on the attitudes of pupils and staff to and within a particular situation.

It is quite difficult to decide in RE what 'facts' a pupil should know. Some things in other areas are obvious, like rules to cross the road, but what 'fact' is crucial in RE? Personally, I do not believe there is one single piece of information that *must* be learned. This is not a statement that nothing should be learned, but that content is relative and the teacher must bear in mind not only the process of learning but also the methods of assessment. One has to take care lest the educational world forgets that the vehicle of assessment and examination only tests how well one can drive the car.

I believe this is not just a practical problem of how to devise effective and comprehensive methods of assessment but also a philosophical issue.

How can any of us judge the effectiveness of what we teach. For example, how can a parent judge whether their son or daughter has been properly brought up? What do we mean by 'brought up'? At what age do we make the assessment: fourteen, twenty-four, eighty-four? In one sense one can never make that assessment, one can only pass a judgement at a given time. I often wonder how contemporaries of Muhammed or Jesus would have assessed them both at twenty years of age. Margaret, the nun who when writing of her decision to enter the cloister commented that her parents felt they had failed, went on to found an Order as well as a popular and successful school in Whitby. Teachers too simply make assessments which are short term, they have no depth of time and yet somehow they do stretch beyond the present.

This needs a little more explanation. All of us, to some extent, have depended upon various assessments made of us in the past. It may be the comment by a teacher that enabled us to get into a higher set, which allowed us to sit for a particular exam, pass it and then move on. Life can be a collection of chances and the accidents may well have a profound effect upon our life. Yet we as teachers recognise that to some extent all our assessments are arbitrary or, at the very least, have an arbitrary sense about them. We all acknowledge that it is easier to mark a pupil down if we do not know them personally. If we know a pupil personally we are also aware of many other factors that impinge on what we hope is an objective assessment. Whenever the teacher makes an assessment it is for *now*, it has a validity for the present, it is made to write on a piece of paper, to talk to another member of staff, to a parent, and most significant of all to the pupil. In this way what the teacher says now about the past has enormous implications for the *future*. Each assessment of a pupil's career or achievement has the quality of an obituary yet this should not be so. Assessment, if it is to be purposeful and positive especially with the pupil who has learning difficulties, has to look to the future and measure the achievements of the pupil against the developing human being.

At the time of writing there appears to be a concerted move to develop the notion of pupil profiles, it may be that over the next fifty years or so the dominant examination system will be replaced by a more detailed and more useful pupil profile. This will minimise the emphasis on written examinations and look more broadly at the whole of the pupil's achievement. This must benefit the pupil with learning problems, as indeed it should benefit all pupils, but it requires teachers to have more time, more space to work on these profiles, because they will need to know their pupils better, teach fewer, and have the opportunity to write longer, more detailed and more reflective comments.

In the chapter on secondary schools much was written about curriculum planning. This is relevant for all schools and not just secondary schools. All those who plan the curriculum must be fully aware of all the balls with which they have to juggle. My own view is that, generally speaking, they have not yet got it right and perhaps one can never expect them to do so. But where they have been imaginative and recognised that the slow learner needs particular support there do appear to be benefits, not only in achievement but in morale. We, as a profession, cannot treat all our pupils in the same way: some require more help and support than others, in a variety of ways. What we must do is to provide a school curriculum which allows us to do our best for each of them and in that sense to treat them equally. It is an important distinction.

It is encouraging to note that in the last few years more local authorities have appointed advisers in Special Education and some have emphasised the importance of Religious Education in this area of schooling. The RE teacher cannot fight battles alone, nor can the head teacher, and resources must be made available from LEAs and the government. The phasing out of ESN(M) schools, or at least their reduction, means that teachers will have to make a real effort to ensure the growing number of pupils with learning difficulties in the 'normal' sector is properly provided for.

All the above really focus on the key issue of coherent planning. If the government encourages the local authorities by releasing special funds directed at the issue, if local authorities make requirements of their schools, if head teachers have the support of their governing bodies and their staff, if the staff plan their lessons properly, then the pupil with learning difficulties will stand a chance. One often hears the term 'positive discrimination', usually used concerning race, colour and women, but if these pupils are to receive a fair deal in the education system then they need a lot of positive discrimination. The links in the chain, alas, leave plenty of scope for weakness though government and local authorities have taken the first steps at least. Teachers will need much more support than they now have if they are to meet this challenge. It is not only support in terms of in-service training and initial training in special services in education, there is a huge shortfall in the number of properly trained and qualified teachers of Religious Education. This has been documented many times over the years but most clearly and damningly in the *RE Directory* (1984) compiled by Dr Brian Gates of St. Martin's College, Lancaster on behalf of the Religious Education Council.

Those who have a concern for RE, indeed those who have read this far, will appreciate that RE is unlikely to be better taught and better resourced if the teachers are not available. One of the conclusions of this investigation is that teachers are being required to develop new skills all the time and this requirement is going to become more essential over the next few years. There are gifted RE teachers, there are gifted teachers of the pupil with learning difficulties, but over the next ten to fifteen years these will have to be blended together.

The one clear positive conclusion that did emerge from the project was that the great aid to all teachers would be more teaching staff. If more teachers were to be made available, then each pupil would have more claim on the teacher's time. This is not a blanket plea for more teachers, however it is a desire to see more teachers with specific responsibility for pupils with learning difficulties in each school and with some freedom with regard to timetabling and the curriculum structure. The temptation for a school if it increased the number of teachers might be to create a general improvement in pupil/teacher ratios across the board, or even give specialist tuition to the very able (also incidentally a neglected group). It seems that at least part of the answer to teaching pupils with learning difficulties lies not simply in smaller classes but more probably in a greater range of teaching strategies and methods being available. This offers the pupil more opportunity to develop new skills and to recognise areas within the curriculum where they may respond more successfully.

Where does RE stand in all of this? Much of the above has been concerned with education but what of religion? If one looks at the waves of development in RE since 1944, the subject generally speaking has passed through a Bible phase, an existential or 'relevance' phase, a world religions phase, a Christianity as a world religion phase, and perhaps in the late 1980s a spirituality phase. Yet none of these have been exclusive. There are still schools which teach only the Bible, others look at 'life issues' and so on. Life is too complex to imagine that any development in RE excludes another, they jumble up and one movement or phase affects another so that there are many different approaches and many different syllabuses. Indeed this may be why the non-specialist teacher looks in bewilderment at what has happened and wonders what to teach. And it is confusing; the aims and objectives style syllabuses of the mid-seventies to late-eighties are not always helpful to the non-specialist teacher. The syllabuses of the 1940s and 1950s with their lists of Bible passages were ironically much more helpful because they laid down what was considered to be essential.

The evidence gathered during the project suggests that to say that 'the teacher must begin where the pupils are' may or may not be true depending on one's interpretation. Certainly the successful teachers begin where the pupils are in terms of methods and resources, but they did not necessarily begin in the vicinity of the pupils' world. Look around the average primary school classroom, projects abound on 'dinosaurs', 'the Romans' and 'the Saxons', none of which are within the pupils' direct experience but are interesting topics in themselves. Similarly with religion, one does not have to start with Christianity – it may well be strange to many pupils. One can start with any religion as long as the method and approach recognise the pupils' abilities.

From observation, it appears that first school RE largely begins with stories, usually about Jesus or other Biblical characters. Teachers tend not, on the whole, to go straight in to the writings of Augustine or the doctrine of the Trinity. It is surprising therefore that some teachers shy away from Hinduism or Islam because of the difficulty of their beliefs and the social structures involved. They too have stories appropriate for 5- to 7-year-olds.

The point is that content is important because it needs to provide good resources upon which a pupil's interest and participation can be developed. More crucial though are the teaching strategies adopted by the teacher and the methods used to put these strategies into effect.

I do wonder whether as an RE profession we have become too obsessed with the minutiae of religious belief and practice, much of which would be unknown by the worshippers themselves. Someone brought up in the Anglican Church, for example, might not recognise what was happening at either end of the Anglican spectrum. And as for asking worshippers the details of their faith in any religion one gets a variety of replies. All of this I find rather comforting because it suggests that religion is not about detail but about experience and feeling. It is the latter which should be transmitted to the pupil, particularly the pupil with learning difficulties. If such an approach cannot be made then one is not teaching RE but a subject more akin to learning mathematical tables by rote – a subject consisting of facts which have no apparent application to reality.

This is easy to suggest but less easy to put into practice, however it would seem to me that from 5 to 14 (the pre-examination age range) much more thought ought to be given to how one creates atmosphere in a classroom. Religions, as mentioned above, are generally concerned to instruct their followers to a greater or lesser degree, but they do so within the context of an atmosphere, a particular ambience which lends itself to learning. Teachers do face a genuine problem here because the commitment a worshipper has to a particular religion cannot be easily taught or understood in the classroom. One could argue that the essence of what it means to be religious is the very area where it is impossible to teach – but there lies another book.

The good teacher is the real key to the problems of the pupil with learning difficulties, not simply a good communicator but one who looks with care at possible reasons why a pupil doesn't seem to be learning. This does involve self-criticism and self-awareness allied to the ability to change direction. It also means not being too ready to diagnose the pupil's problem. All IQ tests have their drawbacks; if people don't understand us we often regard it as their fault not ours, we like to distance ourselves from failure and we easily make judgements about other people. How difficult it is for the pupil who knows little or no success, who lacks confidence, who feels at a loss in the competitive world of a school. The skills of encouragement, of developing a teaching strategy that will not underline the problems of the learner are immense yet these can, and are, developed by the skilled teacher.

Like the pupil, the teacher too can have problems, we all have blind spots, all of us have difficulty learning something. Teachers too can lack imagination, fail to bring out the potential within the pupil, slap down a response because it is not the expected one, attribute bad behaviour to the pupil without thinking the cause might lie in the lesson. The layers are legion and will probably never be completely grasped, but the more the pupil and teacher come to understand and respect each other the better it is for both.

The pattern, common in many schools, of stimulus, discussion and written or formal response appears at face value to inhibit the pupil with learning difficulties. Clarity of aim seems to be crucial for the teacher and this must be related to clarity of instruction – instruction to the pupil of what is required. Then one enters the value-ridden exercise of what acceptable response the pupil may make to the stimulus provided by the teacher. Does the teacher value equally:

(a)	verbal comments	(f)	a general air of interest
(b)	written work	(g)	a comment after the lesson or the next day
(c)	art work		
(d)	drama	(h)	a real effort to produce good work
(e)	model-making		

Is the pupil who has difficulty expressing ideas or responses verbally or in writing always struggling for approval? The care and devotion that went into the pupil's painting of the Tower of London reflected a great commitment not only to the visit but to the art medium and these twin factors focused and coalesced in his work. But can the teacher and the school now identify the pupil as 'intelligent' or 'articulate' or is it just one good piece of work that doesn't make him a bright child? And how does one judge a work of art as good? One simply enters into another complex area of evaluation. Does an excellent piece of work rate as a flash in the pan or is it evidence of real ability lying beneath the surface which the teacher had managed to touch? The danger is always that one accepts the 'average' or the 'norm' so that the corners of achievement may be easily struck down.

These experiences with pupils threw great doubt upon the work of Goldman and Piaget, in fact upon all those who use the written or spoken word as the sole, or even major, method of evaluating a child's level of knowledge and understanding. Time and again it appears that what the pupil lacks is an available channel of communication, so those who use the questionnaire or question and answer technique inhibit these pupils automatically. It must be within the vision of the teacher to see the inherent value of each child and search for methods and processes where that ability can come to light, so that the pupil can recognise achievement and gain in self-confidence and self-respect. The responses of these pupils and others suggests that the failings of the pupil may often be the failing of the teacher and that the term 'slow learner' may be better applied to those teachers who are not innovative and creative, who do not look for more effective means of providing the pupil with the skills of articulating and fulfilling what is within.

Pupils, in my experience, are often more profound than we are willing to allow. As adults and teachers we can and do patronise them, perhaps unconsciously. We put them down (not necessarily just the bright, able pupils) because they challenge us. The pupil with learning difficulties can challenge each of us in a way far beyond what we expect – the 'dissonance factor' disrupts our comfortable, ordered world.

Appendix 1

Audio-visual resources

a list to provoke experiment

This list is prepared with the needs of the pupil with learning difficulties in mind but it is hoped that it may be of value for a wider use. The three theme categories chosen represent current practice in schools and the list is not intended to be exhaustive – only suggestive.

1 Audio materials

Bible

Belshazzar's Feast, Walton. HMV Angel series record. (SAN 324) London Symphony Orchestra and Chorus conducted by André Previn. The Bible story told in a taut and powerful oratorio in 35 minutes. The lamentations of Israel, the judgement on Belshazzar and praise to God are finely interpreted.

The Jesus Programmes 5 cassettes – 10 programmes with supporting leaflets. (Mary Glasgow) News broadcasting styles are used to tell the story of the life of Jesus with interviews, on-the-spot reports and sound effects. The programmes are faithful to the Bible text.

Noah and the Ark Cassette and book. (Macdonald)
Daniel in the Lions' Den Cassette and book. (Macdonald)
Jonah and the Great Fish Cassette and book. (Macdonald)
David and Goliath Cassette and book. (Macdonald)

The Parable of the Good Samaritan Cassette, music book and teaching notes. (Trim Publications, 1 Argyle Road, Bognor Regis, PO21 1DY) The Good Samaritan told on cassette with specially written music and songs for juniors.

Two Stories Jesus Told Ladybird book, cassette and colouring book. Derek Nimmo reads the book with some musical accompaniment.

Three Parables Cassette and booklet. (Angel Press)

Tell me the Stories of Jesus Cassette. (National Christian Education Council)

The Happy Shepherds Cassette and booklet. (Church House Publishing)

Implicit

The Four Seasons, Vivaldi. Classics for Pleasure record. (CFP 40016) The Virtuosi of England – Kenneth Sillito, violin. Spring, summer, autumn and winter are described in music of great beauty.

Now You See Me, Now You Don't, Cliff Richard. Record. (EMI EMC 3415) A recent collection of songs by a Christian artist in which most of the lyrics have subtle religious connections. One is a Christmas hymn 'Little Town', and another 'Son of Thunder' has biographical elements.

Simon and Garfunkel's Greatest Hits Record. (CBS S69003) Includes 'The Sound of Silence' and 'Bridge over Troubled Water' amongst other numbers which reflect approaches to basic contemporary issues.

Voices First Book/Record Two. (Argo PLP 1113) Part of an anthology of recorded sounds, music, songs and speech presented by Geoffrey Summerfield in association with Penguin Education.

World religions

Enjoy Chanukah at Home, Michael Goulston. Cassette and notes. This Eiber production offers a varied audio picture of the festival and the first side includes the dramatised story, a blessing and a Rabbinic debate. The second side has eight parts to be used by Jewish families on each night of the festival.

Godspell Record. (Bells 203) The London cast recording of the musical based on St. Matthew's Gospel.

Missa Luba Record. (Philips BL 7592) This is a Mass sung in pure Congolese style without western musical influences and is sung by Les Troubadours du Roi Baudouin. Part of the music was used in the film 'If'.

Music in the World of Islam 1. The Human Voice Record. (Tangent TGS 131) Part of an anthology of music throughout the Islamic world in which the human voice is the foundation of all music. Few of the recordings are made in studio conditions.

Religions of the Middle East – Christian, Jewish, Islamic, produced by Deben Bhattacharya. Record. (Argo ZFB 54) A varied collection ranging from the bells of Nazareth to Dervish dances with Hebrew readings and prayers. There is a strong atmosphere of devotion and faith.

2 Slides

Bible

The Life and Teaching of Jesus – 2. Jesus the Teacher 12 colour slides. Photos. (Lion) Pictures of places, people and artefacts with notes that draw out Bible links, and a small map.

Terres Saintes, Terres Vivantes – B. Agricultural Work 18 colour slides. Photos. (ACNAV, 3 Rue Amyot, 75005 Paris) Excellent quality photographs of shepherds and the harvesting and processing of corn. Notes are in French.

Zaccheus 12 colour slides. Artwork. (Docete Foundation) The story is told by brightly coloured slides drawn in a simple style. Commentary provided is in Dutch.

Implicit

Exploring the Cosmos 12 colour slides. Photos. (Cassette available). (Ealing Abbey/Farmington Trust) A group of photograph of quality designed to encourage children to explore creation, the exploration of space and the use of resources.

Faces 12 colour slides. Photos. (Slide Centre) The compilers have succeeded in gathering a wide selection of portraits from infancy to old age. Individuals and groups are represented.

The Language of Signs 16 colour slides. Photos. (Slide Centre) A varied collection of pictures of signs designed to stimulate creative thinking about the environment and the richness of symbolism.

Pollution 12 colour slides. Photos. (Slide Centre) Visual and material pollution are represented on these slides.

World religions

Christian Initiation – Infant Baptism & Confirmation (People at Worship) 21 colour slides. Photos. (Slide Centre) Two churches in Leicester are the settings for the Anglican rites of Baptism and Confirmation from the Alternative Service Book. Notes are provided.

Hindu Worship (People at Worship) 24 colour slides. Photos. (Slide Centre) The worship takes place in a temple in Leicester which was formerly a Baptist church. Notes are provided and the set provides a useful view of a Hindu community in this country.

Islam the Way of Peace 34 colour slides and cassette – 10 minutes. (The Islamic Foundation) A mixture of photos and diagrams is used to give an outline of the main Islamic teachings and to show something of the life style of Muslims.

Living Judaism 67 colour slides and cassette – 21 minutes. Photos. (Council of Christians & Jews, 1 Dennington Park Road, London NW6) An account of Judaism designed to enable Christians to understand something of the religion. Background information is given but the emphasis is on current practices. Full notes are provided.

3   Filmstrips

Bible

The Champion S/st, colour, artwork. (Scripture Union) Six 3½-minute cartoon sequences covering the Easter story, each lasting the length of a song by Garth Hewitt.

He's Here – 8: Outside the City S/st, colour, photos. (Church Army) The eighth in a nine-part series (14-minutes in length) covering the life of Jesus using children for the characters. This part focuses on the Crucifixion.

Luke Street S/st, colour, artwork. (Scripture Union) Eight 4-minute sequences on two filmstrips, telling stories from the Gospels.

Implicit

Freedom to Fly: a Seagull F/st, colour, photos. (St. Paul's) Colour photographs of a seagull in flight. Also available are a record of the same title, and a book entitled *Jonathan Livingstone Seagull.*

Me! F/st, colour, photos. (Philip Green Ed Ltd.) A filmstrip focusing on the self, others, similarities and differences, feeling, and taking care of self and others.

Religious Expression S/st, colour, photos. (Argus) A soundstrip, also available as part of the multi-media pack *Religious Expression Unit* in the Religion in Human Culture Series, which focuses on visible expressions of religion through buildings, symbols, social involvement etc.

World religions

A Jewish Family Event – Barmitzvah F/st, colour, photos. (Central Jewish Lecture & Information Committee) The events leading up to and including the Barmitzvah ceremony.

Rites of Passage – Initiation S/st, colour, photos. (Mary Glasgow) The second in a four part series which explores the rituals associated with major events in the cycle of life.

4 Posters

Bible

Il Figlio Prodigo – Il Padre Perdona (Elle Di Ci) Available from St. Paul's Book Centre. A set of eight Italian posters which cover the parable of the prodigal son. Colour is used to evoke the mood of the picture.

Life of Jesus Mafa (Methodist Church Overseas Division) Three sets of colour drawings are available, each showing ten different scenes from the Gospel as dramatised by the Mafa people of North Cameroun.

The Pieta (St. Paul's Book Centre) A photograph of the famous marble sculpture of The Pieta. Many posters are available of famous works of art, e.g. Athena, Medici, the National Gallery.

Veritas Bible Pictures – Pack 1, Geoffrey Chapman. A selection of nine colour posters illustrating Bible themes.

The Wise Men Follow the Star, Mayhew McCrimmon. A set of four posters selected from the illustrations to the book of the same title. Also available in each title of *The King's Donkey Series* is a jigsaw puzzle and a set of workcards.

Implicit

Foto Symboliche 9 (Elli Di Ci) One of the Italian sets of black and white pictures on a variety of themes. A wide selection of packs is available (Elli Di Ci and Du Chalet) from St. Paul's Book Centre, providing useful talking points.

Children Around the World Pack of 16 different posters. (Macmillan)

The Human Face of Development (UNICEF, 46 Osnaburgh Street, London NW1) A set of eight colour posters with a brownish hue which illustrates different aspects of development. No captions are given, but included are some very evocative close-ups.

People Who Help Us –1 Pack of 12 black and white posters. (Philip Green Educational Ltd.)

The Natural Wonders of the World (Macmillan) A beautiful pack of 16 charts showing some of the natural wonders of the world, including the Himalayas, the Grand Canyon, the Iguassu Falls in Brazil and Ayers Rock in Australia.

Parish Posters (USPG) Parish Posters are available through a mailing system in sets of four. They are black and white, with captions.

The Terraced House Books Poster Sets (Methuen) Everyday pictures of Asian families – the new baby, a Sikh shopkeeper, a mother in the kitchen, and the clinic.

Trees of Europe Through the Four Seasons (Argus) A boxed set of 92 colour posters showing 24 different trees through the four seasons. Sample packs are also available of individual tree species.

Ways of Seeing – Trees Posters and notes. (PCET)

World religions

CEM Colour Posters – Christianity (Christian Education Movement) Included in the folder are six posters illustrating different aspects of Christianity – a Quaker wedding, a family saying Grace, social involvement, an Orthodox priest, a coffee bar, and a sculpture.

Festivals Around the World (Macmillan) A pack containing six charts including the Dogan Dancers of Mali, the Chinese New Year, and the Bun Festival of Hong Kong.

Major World Religions – Judaism (Argus) Two colour posters, with captions, on Judaism, one giving the Star of David symbol and the other showing an orthodox Jew praying at the Western Wall. Available also in a set of 18 posters on Major World Religions.

My Neighbour's Religion (Pictorial Charts Educational Trust) One large chart illustrating six major world religions – Hinduism, Sikhism, Judaism, Islam, Christianity and Buddhism. Notes on the chart are also included.

5   Transmissions

Bible

(a)   Radio:

Religious Education – the Life of Jesus – Vocation (BBC Radio for Schools) One of a series of 20-minute radio broadcasts 'Religious Education' for 13- to 16-year-olds. In this series on the 'Life of Jesus' the programme 'Vocation' uses dramatisation and interviews interspersed with narration.

(b)   Video:

Jesus of Nazareth – Part 4 (Precision Video, 19 Upper Brook Street, London W1Y 1PD) 103 minutes. Zeffirelli's film was originally transmitted on television but is now available in 4 parts. Normally it would be purchased from retailers.

(c)   BBC Radiovision:

How the Bible Came to Us 39 double frame filmstrip. Colour photos.

(BBC/Longman) A Radiovision production for which the sound-track of 20 minutes is broadcast. Aimed at 9- to 11-year-olds the story of the transmission of the Bible is told.

Implicit

(a) Radio:

Contact – Material for Primary Assemblies – A World Without Colour (BBC Radio for Schools) A 10-minute radio broadcast intended for primary school assemblies. *A World Without Colour* tells the amusing tale of a 'colourless' character who was a 'viewer' not a 'doer', and could only see the world in 'black and white'.

(b) Video:

An Everyday Miracle (BBC General Studies) Suitable for 16- to 18-year-olds – 25 mins. The development of the human embryo in the womb is shown in remarkable pictures with commentary spoken by David Attenborough.

Kids Can Say No Video. (Rolf Harris Video, 43 Drury Lane, London WC2B 5RT)

(c) BBC Radiovision:

Signs of Life 36 double frame filmstrip. Colour photos. (BBC) Radiovision programme supplied with notes although 20 minutes soundtrack is to be recorded off air. Symbolism is touched on in general terms and the use of signs and symbols in five major religions is illustrated.

World Religions

(a) Radio:

Religious Education – Places of Pilgrimage – Mecca (BBC Radio for Schools) A series of radio broadcasts focusing on famous places of pilgrimage – Canterbury, Lourdes, Benares, Jerusalem and Mecca. Narration and interviews combine to tell the story of the pilgrimage to Mecca. Intended for 13- to 16-year-olds.

(b) Video:

Worship (Believe It Or Not series) 15 minutes. (ITV Schools) A view of worship in a number of faiths designed for secondary schools. Most of the material comes from the Midlands.

Christianity Through the Eyes of Christian Children Video. (CEM)
Judaism Through the Eyes of Jewish Children Video. (CEM)
Sikhism Through the Eyes of Sikh Children Video. (CEM)
Hinduism Through the Eyes of Hindu Children Video. (CEM)

Quakerism Through the Eyes of Quaker Children Video. (CEM)
Islam Through the Eyes of Muslim Children Video. (CEM)

(c)   BBC Radiovision:

Sacred Books 29 double frame filmstrip. Colour photos. (BBC)
Another Radiovision programme offering an introduction to the
sacred books of five religions. Useful background material is given
for each religion.

Appendix 2

Children with learning difficulties: selected titles

This list is intended to offer help to the many teachers who are concerned with the religious education of children with learning difficulties. Background material and practical handbooks are to be found together with a selection of resources to be used with pupils. The list is primarily designed for use in the maintained schools but Christian nurture is included and the contribution of Roman Catholics in this field may especially be noted.

1 Background reading/theory

Children with Special Needs in the Infants' School, Lesley Webb. (Collins, 1974) A wide variety of special needs are identified and considered, including withdrawn/aggressive/anxious/bizarre behaviour. Children with physical limitations and cultural differences are discussed.

The Deaf Child and his Family, Susan Gregory. (Allen & Unwin, 1976) Based on over one hundred interviews with mothers of deaf children, this book describes everyday life and activities within the family. The effects of the disability on family life and modes of coping with the problems are shown.

The Education of Slow Learning Children, A. E. Tansley and R. Gulliford (Routledge & Kegan Paul, 1965) A summary of the intellectual, emotional and physical characteristics of retarded children related to teaching methods within the classroom.

The Mentally Retarded Child, Abraham Levinson. (Allen & Unwin, 1967) An updated guide for parents dealing with basic issues such as diagnosis, causes and treatment of mental retardation. There is a chapter on education.

2   The handicapped in the community

Colours of Day (Liverpool Catholic Social Services, 150 Brownlow Hill, Liverpool L3 5RF, 1980) A pamphlet of practical suggestions for those working alongside handicapped people.

What Is It Like To Be Me?, edited by Helen Exley. (Exley Publications, 1981) An anthology of words and pictures written and illustrated entirely by disabled children.

3   Reports and case studies

The Curriculum in Special Schools, M. D. Wilson. (Longman, 1981) Schools Council Programme 4. Current practice, rationale, constraints and resources in special education, with comments on the future.

Mixed Ability Work in Comprehensive Schools (HMSO, 1978) An HMI discussion paper including sections on children with disabilities and specific comments related to religious education.

Recent Curriculum Development in Special Education, Seamus Hegarty. (Longman, 1982) Schools Council Programme 4. Examples of curricular development in special schools in England and Wales.

Religious and Moral Education of Deaf Children (General Synod Council for the Deaf, CIO, 1976) The report of a church working party based on a wide circulation of questionnaires and recognising that 'many will carry into adulthood their linguistic, communicative, psychological and emotional problems'.

This report led to a further report published in 1979: *Report of the Working Party on the Religious Education and Moral Education of Deaf Young People*. This contains suggestions for a syllabus, with resources, and considers such issues as the role of worship, and gives advice and guidance for the home.

Religious Education in Special Schools – a Report, Jean Richardson. (CEM, 1979) An exploration of the place of religious education in the curriculum of special schools, which should encourage experimental programmes.

Working with Mentally Handicapped People (National Youth Bureau, 1980) A loose-leaf folder on community involvement by young people, including 8 case studies, a checklist for organisers and a list of resource agencies.

4 Practical handbooks for teachers

RE Handbook (Scripture Union) A resource book of Christian nurture for primary school teachers produced in a magazine style. Undated material is provided for each term based on Christian festivals and Bible characters. The set of worksheets may be duplicated for group use.

Teaching Christianity, Mabel Hayes. (Mowbray, 1982–1985) A series based on parish work, providing resource and lesson books including worksheets for duplicating. Two resource books and four lesson books have been published in this series.

Teaching Mentally Handicapped Children, Barabara Brooks. (Ward Lock Educational, 1978) A practical handbook of suggestions for a stimulating curriculum of physical and creative activities. Helpful tips are provided on other practical topics, and classroom testing and discussion themes are also included.

The Bible in the Classroom: No. 4 – Teaching the Bible to Slow Learners, Sue Phillips. (NS/BRF) One in a series of four leaflets, available as a set, on different aspects of teaching the Bible. Hints are given on seeing beyond the story and dealing with abstract concepts.

5 A further reading list for teachers with a special interest in the British situation

'The Religious Education of the Retarded: a Symposium', B. H. Arkebauer *et al. Religious Education* Vol. LX (1965)
Catechetical Pedagogy of the Mentally Deficient Child, Henri Bissonnier. (Lumen Vitae Press, Brussels, 1962)
'For the "Slow Learner" . . . God is not an Abstraction', Henri Bissonnier. *Learning for Living* Vol. 14 No. 3 (1975)
The Education of Dull Children at the Secondary Stage, Cheshire Education Committee. (University of London, 1963)
Number Unknown: a Guide to the Needs and Problems of the Mentally Sub-normal Child and his Family, Children's Council. (Church Information Office, 1965)
Teaching the Slow Learner in the Primary School, M. F. Cleugh. (Methuen, London, 1961)
Invitation to Communion, S. Clifford. (Kevin Mayhew Publishers, 1980)
An Investigation into the Development of Certain Religious Concepts in ESN Children, J. Cope. (Unpublished Dissertation, Liverpool, Dip. T.H.C., 1967)

'Honest to Goldman: an Assessment', E. Cox, *Religious Education* Vol. LXIII No. 6 (1968)

RE Course for the Mentally Handicapped, edited by Sister Jean Daniel. (Mayhew–McCrimmon, Great Wakering, 1977)

All Children are Special: The Religious Needs of Educationally Subnormal Children, edited by A. H. Denney. (Church Information Office for the Children's Council of the Church of England, 1967)

The Special Child, B. Furneaux. (Penguin Books, 1969)

Special Educational Needs, R. Gulliford. (Routledge & Kegan Paul, London, 1971)

Religion and Slow Learners: a Research Study, K. E. Hyde. (SCM Press, 1969)

Learning for Living, a special issue of *Religious Education and the Slow Learner* Vol. 14 No. 3 (1975)

'The Religious Education of Backward Children: A Symposium'. *Religion in Education* Vol. 37 (1959)

'Retarded Child and Religious Education: A Case Study', D. J. Silver, *Religious Education* Vol. LII (1957)

'Religion and the Handicapped Child', E. R. Stair. *Religious Education* Vol. LXII (1967)

6   Workcards to use with the children

Basic Bible 1: Learning about Jesus. (Bible Society) A kit for use in the primary classroom, with which children can work at their own pace. Included are story cards, worksheets, find out cards, and display posters.

Visions 1, 2, 3, 4, compiled by Ian Wragg *et al.* (Lutterworth, 1977/81) Loose-leaf packs of workcards on a wide variety of themes, using short stories, discussion starters, cartoon strips and line drawings with suggested related activities.

7   Cartoon-style presentation of material

The Apostles – their Story in Pictures and *Jesus – his Story in Pictures*, Peter Mullen and Martin Pitts. (Edward Arnold, 1980 and 1979) Two titles in a series of books presenting the New Testament story in cartoon strips. Unobtrusive questions are included at the bottom of a page and these may be used as discussion starters.

From Slave to Star and *Samson the Mighty*. (Bible Society, 1979) Colourful comic stories from the Old Testament. The text of the Good News Bible is used and the comic includes the printed story. Key events are presented in typical comic style.

Picture Bible: New Testament. (Scripture Union/Ark Publishing, 1981) The Gospel and Acts in picture strips with a selection of illustrations from the teaching of Paul and others.

Note: From time to time publishers produce cartoon-style Bible stories e.g. Lion, Hodder & Stoughton. Various American type comics may also appear, on contemporary characters e.g. *The Hiding Place*.

8   Pupils' texts and story books

Bobbi's New Year, Joan Solomon. (Hamish Hamilton, 1980) The Joan Solomon series uses colour photographs with a short, clear text to describe people from different ethnic groups and their special celebrations.

The Christian Adventure (series), H. G. Moses. (Blond Educational) A traditional textbook on the Bible in which the clear presentation of the story with simple follow-up work could be useful.

Claire and Emma, Diana Peter. (A. and C. Black, 1976) One in a series of books which focus on people with particular handicaps. Colourful pictures with a short text.

Faith in Action (series). (RMEP) A series of booklets providing short stories on the lives of famous Christians. These include:

Devil's Island, Brian Peachment. (1974) The story of Charles Pean and the prison island.
Escape From Death, Douglas Hare. (1978) The Story of Sundar Singh.
Island of No Return, Geoffrey Hanks. (1978) Father Damien and the leper colony.
The Nun in The Concentration Camp, G. W. Target. (1974) Mother Maria at Ravensbruck.
The Tiger of Naples, Brian Peachment. (1978) Father Borrelli and the children of Naples.

Other stories focus on ethnic minorities and friendships between the races:

Go Well, Stay Well, Toeckey Jones. (Fontana/Collins, 1982) The friendship of a black and a white girl in South Africa.
My Mate Shofiq, Jan Needle. (Fontana/Collins, 1979)
The Friends, Rosa Guy. (Victor Gollancz, 1979)

9   Assembly books

Assembly books provide a valuable resource of stories and fables from around the world. See particularly:

Assembly Stories from Around the World, William Dargue. (OUP, 1983)
Focus, Redvers Brandling. (Bell and Hyman, 1983)
101 School Assembly Stories and *A Second Book of 101 School Assembly Stories*,
Frank Carr. (W. Foulsham and Co. 1973 and 1981)
Themework, John Bailey. (Stainer and Bell, 1981)
How a Hindu/Moslem/Sikh/Roman Catholic Prays (Minority Group Support
Service, Southfields Old School, South Street, Hillfields, Coventry)
Short pamphlets to illustrate prayer in the different religions. Pictures are
photocopied, with a clear, short text on the adjoining page. Not the best
of reproductions but a useful addition in this subject area.

The National Society's RE Centre has a comprehensive up-to-date list.

10   A short age-referenced list for use in the classroom

5+	*One Night at a Time*, S. Hill. (Hamish Hamilton, 1984)
5+	*Pit Holiday*, I. Menter. (Hamish Hamilton, 1986)
5+	*Anna*, M. Wadhams. (Bodley Head, 1986)
5+	*Tom Visits the Dentist*, N. Snell. (Hamish Hamilton, 1979)
5+	*Peter Gets a Hearing Aid*, N. Snell. (Hamish Hamilton, 1979)
10+	*Religions*, R. Fisher. (Macdonald, 1987)
10+	*Book of Prayers*, H. Slater. (Macdonald, 1987)
5+	*Why a Donkey was Chosen*, C. Gregorowski. (Ernest Benn, 1979)
10+	*Jesus and the Kingdom*, S. Phillips. (Longman, 1986)
10+	*Christianity in Words and Pictures*, S. Thorley. (RMEP, 1984)
10+	*Judaism in Words and Pictures*, S. Thorley. (RMEP, 1986)
10+	*Islam in Words and Pictures*, S. Thorley. (RMEP, 1982)
5+	*All Things Bright and Beautiful*, P. Baynes. (Lutterworth, 1986)
10+	My Belief (series) I am a(n) . . .! Anglican, Roman Catholic, Jew, Sikh, Muslim, Hindu, Greek Orthodox, Buddhist, Rastafarian. (Franklin Watts, 1986)
5+	*Butterfly and Caterpillar*, B. Watts. (A. and C. Black, 1985)
5+	*Discovering Colours*, M. Fergus. (Lion, 1974)
10+	*Tom and Maggie*, D. Horgan. (OUP, 1986)
10+	*Toymaker's Workshop*, R. Broome. (NCEC, 1986)
10+	*What Are You Scared Of?*, H. Larsen. (A. and C. Black, 1979)
5+	*Danny is Afraid of the Dark*, N. Snell. (Hamish Hamilton, 1982)
10+	*Mummy Goes into Hospital*, E. Elliot. (Hamish Hamilton, 1985)
10+	*Wheelchair Summer*, D. Oxley. (Lion, 1981)
5+	*Suzy*, E. Chapman. (Bodley Head, 1982)
5+	*Rachel*, E. Fanshawe. (Bodley Head, 1975)
5+	*The Boy Who Couldn't Hear*, F. Bloom. (Bodley Head, 1977)
5+	*Don't Forget Tom*, H. Larsen. (A. and C. Black, 1974)

Mealtime With Lily (ILEA Learning Resources)
Going to the Park (ILEA Learning Resources)
Saiqua and Shan Go Shopping (ILEA Learning Resources)
Keven and Lee Play Together (ILEA Learning Resources)
Changing Baby Hollie (ILEA Learning Resources)
Bedtime with Alcan (ILEA Learning Resources)
Eating with Badre and Nabil (ILEA Learning Resources)
Rashan Gets Dressed (ILEA Learning Resources)
Bathtime With Leanda (ILEA Learning Resources)

The above ILEA books are excellent spiral picture books – no script – with laminated pages. Originally published for use in language programmes for children with learning difficulties, the lack of text and multi-faith content makes them an ideal addition to all classrooms and age ranges.

11   Illustrated Bible stories

Ladybird Bible Stories and *Ladybird Bible Books* (series, large format) (Ladybird)
Listen! and *Praise!*, A. J. McCallen. (Collins 1976, 1979)
New World and *Winding Quest*, A. T. Dale. (OUP, 1976, 1974)
A Visual New/Old Testament/Story of Christianity, A. G. Patson. (RMEP, 1974–75)

These books show the variety of approaches that are used in illustrating the Bible.

12   Stories about handicapped children

The Trouble with Donovan Croft, Bernard Ashley. (Oxford University Press, 1974) Loss of speech.

The Witch's Daughter, Nina Bawden. (London, Gollancz, 1973) Blindness.

The Four of Us, Elizabeth Beresford. (London, Hutchinson, 1981) Mental handicap.

Alexander in Trouble, Susan Burke. (London, Bodley Head, 1979) Wheel chair.

The Finn Bequest, Kim Chesher. (London, Hamish Hamilton, 1978) Blindness.

Burnish Me Bright, Julia Cunningham. (London, Heinemann, 1971) Muteness.

Annerton Pit, Peter Dickinson. (London, Gollancz, 1977) Blindness.

Mum on Wheels, Hazel Edwards. (London, Hodder & Stoughton, 1980) Wheel chair.

The Summer House Loon, Anne Fine. (London, Methuen, 1978) Blindness.

The Bright and Morning Star, Rosemary Harris. (London, Faber & Faber, 1972) Deafness.

The Namesake, C. Walter Hodges. (London, Bell, 1964) Loss of leg.

Head Over Wheels, Lee Kingman. (London, Hamish Hamilton, 1978) Wheel chair.

Don't Forget Tom, Hanne Larsen. (London, A. and C. Black, 1972) Brain damage.

The Young Unicorns, Madeleine L'Engle. (London, Gollancz, 1969) Blindness.

White Hope, Frances Murray. (London, Hodder & Stoughton, 1978) Physical deformity.

Sally Can't See, Palle Petersen. (London, A. & C. Black, 1975) Blindness.

David in Silence, Veronica Robinson. (London, Deutsch, 1965) Deafness.

Martin Rides the Moor, Vian Smith. (Kestrel Books, 1980) Deafness.

Let the Balloon Go, Ivan Southall. (London, Methuen, 1968) Spastic.

The Nothing-space, Eleanor Spence. (London, OUP, 1972) Deafness.

The October Child, Eleanor Spence. (Oxford University Press, 1976) Autism.

Warrior Scarlet, Rosemary Sutcliff. (Oxford University Press, 1958) Loss of use of arm.

The Witch's Brat, Rosemary Sutcliff. (Oxford University Press, 1970) Physical deformity.

The Cay, Theodore Taylor. (London, Heineman, 1969) Blindness.

Janet at School, Paul White. (London, A. and C. Black, 1978) Spina bifida.

A Friendship of Equals, Gina Wilson. (London, Faber & Faber, 1981) Wheel chair.

I Own the Racecourse, Patricia Wrightson. (London, Hutchinson, 1968) Mental handicap.

What Difference Does it Make, Danny?, Helen Young. (London, Deutsch, 1980) Epilepsy.

13 Education in the church

(a) Anglican materials

Preparing the Mentally Handicapped for Confirmation, John Bradford. (Church of England Children's Society, 1981) Prepared for the International Year of Disabled People, this discussion paper faces issues raised by this subject. The preparation and the service itself are covered and suggestions are made for the follow-up and integration of the candidate into the church.

Share the Word 1 and 2, and *This is the Life*. (Catholic Information Office, 1980) Here are just two approaches to Sunday School material. Many practical activities are suggested for the three age groups – children, young people, and adults, which could suitably be adapted for those with learning difficulties.

(b) Roman Catholic materials

Catechesis of the Mentally Handicapped, Kevin Nichols. (Catholic Information Office, 74 Gallows Hill Lane, Abbots Langley, Herts.) A leaflet detailing ideas and proposals for the catechesis of the mentally handicapped, and how they relate to and are received into the Church.

The Gospel for Children, Bruna Battistella. (St. Paul, 1981) Colourful sketch drawings with simple text, presenting (a) the Gospel Story, (b) the Teaching of Jesus, and (c) the Church Community.

I Am With You, edited by D. C. Wilson. (St. Paul, 1975) An introduction to the religious education of the mentally handicapped in the church school, the home and the parish. A valuable book by one of the leading Roman Catholic practitioners in the field.

Invitation to Communion, Sister Stephanie Clifford. (Kevin Mayhew, 1980) A first communion programme for mentally handicapped children.

Learning to Pray with the Mentally Handicapped ('Getting in touch with God' series), Sister Jean. (Kevin Mayhew, 1981) A booklet of suggestions for praying with the mentally handicapped.

Life to the Full (Guidelines No. 1 Education in Faith), edited by Sister Stephanie Clifford. (St Joseph's Centre, The Burroughs, Hendon NW4, 1980) The catechesis of the mentally handicapped with a programme of 13 sessions focusing on the eucharistic Liturgy.

Notes of Guidance to Help Parents of Mentally Handicapped Children to Prepare them for First Holy Communion. (Salford Diocese Catholic

Handicapped Children's Fellowship) Guidelines for parents in developing a child's senses in the context of preparation for communion – a sense of the world around him and a sense of God the creator.

RE Course for the Mentally Handicapped, Sister Jean Daniel. (Westminster RE Centre) A one-year course for the mentally handicapped.

(c)   Other materials

Christianity and the Mentally Handicapped, Michael Miles. (Paternoster Press, 1978) Occasional Paper No. 7, from the Christian Brethren Research Fellowship. Theological considerations, achievements, opportunities for action and bibliography are included.

How Shall We Care?, L. H. Duncan. (Church of Scotland Dept. of Education, 1980) A practical book to help parents and all those concerned with raising and training handicapped children, including discussion on the role of the church and professional and voluntary agencies.

Appendix 3

Useful addresses

Mailings

The Shap Mailing consists of an annual Calendar of Religious Festivals, details of Shap courses and a booklet of articles (on a specific theme each year). Available from:

The Shap Working Party	*or*	The Shap Working Party
'Mailing' distributor		The Secretary
Mr Peter Woodward		c/o Bishop Otter College
7 Alderbrooke Road		College Lane
Solihull		Chichester
West Midlands B91 1NH		West Sussex PO19 4PE

Religious Education Centre Media Review with 3 mailings despatched to subscribers at the end of the Autumn, Spring and Summer terms. It provides an evaluation of recently published RE resources and also helps to keep teachers aware of the latest developments in the field plus information on courses.

Media Review
The Secretary
RE In-Service Training and Resource Centre
West London Institute of Higher Education
Lancaster House
Borough Road
Isleworth TW7 5DU

Christian Education Movement has a variety of mailings for primary and secondary schools and also publishes the *British Journal of Religious Education*. The price depends upon the type of mailing taken. CEM have a catalogue of the resources they have produced for schools.

Christian Education Movement
Lancaster House
Borough Road
Isleworth
Middlesex TW7 5DU

Resource also has 3 termly mailings and consists of articles, news items and reviews.

Resource
The Secretary
The Dept. of Arts Education
The University of Warwick
Westwood
Coventry CV4 8EE

SMILE Centre offers a wide variety of learning materials for pupils covering mainly mathematics though they have a wider use. They produce a half-termly magazine *Splash.*

SMILE Centre
Middle Row School
Kensal Road
London W10 5DB

Buddhist

The Buddhist Society
58 Eccleston Square
London SW1V 1PH

Clive Erricker
Department of Religious Studies
King Alfred's College
Sparkford Road
Winchester SO22 4NR

Christian

Christian Aid
PO Box No. 1
London SW1

British and Foreign Bible Society
146 Queen Victoria Street
London EC4V 4BX

The National Society's RE
Development Centre
23 Kensington Square
London W8 5HN

Hindu

India House
Aldwych
London WC2
Films available.

Indian Government Tourist Office
7 Cork Street
London W1

Hindu Centre
39 Grafton Terrace
London NW5

Jewish

Rabbi Douglas Charing
Jewish Education Bureau
8 Westcombe Avenue
Leeds LS8 2BS
Has a catalogue of material available
for schools.

Steve Polak
Education Officer
Central Jewish Lecture and
Information Committee
Woburn House
Upper Woburn Place
London WC1H 0EP

Jewish National Fund
Harold Poster House
Kingsbury Circle
London NW9 9SP

Muslim

The Islamic Foundation
233 London Road
Leicester

Mr R. El-Droubie
Minaret House
9 Leslie Park Road
Croydon CR0 6TN

The Muslim Book Shop
233 Seven Sisters Road
London N4

The Islamic Cultural Centre
146 Park Road
London NW8 7RG

Sikh

Sikh Cultural Society
88 Mollison Way
Edgeware
Middlesex HA8 5QW

Sikh Missionary Society
10 Featherstone Road
Southall
Middlesex

India House
(for address see 'Hindu')

Indian Government Tourist Office
(for address see 'Hindu')

An extensive list may also be found in *The Shap Handbook on World Religions in Education* (C.R.E. 1987) and *Living Together* – the handbook for the Birmingham Agreed Syllabus.

Please remember to send a stamped addressed envelope when writing to these organisations.

When in London people may find a visit to the *St. Paul Book Centre* useful, not only for Christian (particularly Catholic material) but also for a good selection of non-confessional books for use in county schools.

St. Paul Book Centre
199 Kensington High Street
London W8 6BA

This is only a short distance from the *Commonwealth Institute* which also has some interesting material for use in school and very close to *The National Society's RE Development Centre*.

Appendix 4

Members of compiling group for chapter 3

Brian Beattie   RE Adviser, Diocesan Education Office, 53 New Street, Chelmsford, Essex CM1 1NG.

Alan Brown   RE (Schools) Officer, General Synod Board of Education, Church House, Dean's Yard, Westminster, London SW1P 3NZ.
Director, The National Society's RE Centre, 23 Kensington Square, London W8 5HN.

Nicky Crane   Ingfield Manor School (Spastics, ESN), Billingshurst, Sussex.

Jill Davies   Advisory Teacher, ILEA.

John Eardley   Director of Education, Coventry Diocese, Leamington Hastings Vicarage, Marton, Rugby, Warwickshire CV23 8EL.

Wyn Ellis   Hawkesbury Fields ESN(S) School, Alderman's Green Road, Coventry, Warwickshire.

Florence Elsey   St. Christopher's School, Thornton Heath, Surrey.

Penny Lacey   Hawkesbury Fields ESN(S) School, Alderman's Green Road, Coventry, Warwickshire.

Penny Lambert   Braybrooke School, Bracknell, Berkshire.

Duncan McGibbon   Jack Tizard ESN(S) School, Finlay Street, London SW6.

Chris Pachter   11 Bourdon Road, Penge, London SE20.

Jill Pagano   St. Nicolas School, Purley, Surrey.

Jim Polland	Chartfield School (Delicate), St. Margaret's Crescent, Roehampton, London SW15.
Sister Gillian Price	St. Elizabeth's School, Much Hadham, Hertfordshire SG10 6EW
Pamela Shaw	St. Nicolas School, Purley, Surrey.
Gay Tsaoussis	St. Christopher's School, Thornton Heath, Surrey.
Paul Turton	Former Director of The National Society's RE Centre, 23 Kensington Square, London W8 5HN.

Index